First Comes Faith

First Comes Faith
Proclaiming the Gospel in the Church

W. Frank Harrington

Geneva Press
Louisville, Kentucky

Scripture quotations from the New Revised Standard Version of the Bible are copyright ©1989 by the Division of Christian Education of the National Council of the Churches of Christ in the U.S.A. and are used by permission.

Book design by Type Shoppe II
Cover design by Jennifer Cox

First edition
Published by Geneva Press
Louisville, Kentucky

This book is printed on acid-free paper that meets the American National Standards Institute Z39.48 standard. ∞

PRINTED IN THE UNITED STATES OF AMERICA
98 99 00 01 02 03 04 05 06 — 10 9 8 7 6 5 4 3 2 1

Library of Congress Cataloging-in-Publication Data

Harrington, W. Frank, 1935–
    First comes faith / W. Frank Harrington.
            p.   cm.
        Includes bibliographical references.
        ISBN 0-664-50017-X
        1. Mission of the church.   I. Title.
    BV601.8.H37   1998
    269—dc21   98-6868

Contents

I dedicate this book to the men and women of Peachtree
Presbyterian Church. We have journeyed together for 27
years. It is their encouragement, loyalty, and prayers
that have sustained the freshness of my call to the ministry.
". . . The saints among us owe much of the remarkable
character of their lives to their sense of God's reality at work
in their lives. Many talk as though no day is so ordinary or
commonplace but that God is in it. In driving to work, caring
for sick loved ones, accomplishing the thousand and one
tasks of daily life, they find a dimension of the transcendent
that lends a special character to how they live. . . ."*
I have walked among such people at Peachtree.

*Gallup, George H. Jr., and Timothy Jones, *The Saints Among Us*

Acknowledgments

The Bible says that "of the making of books there is no end," and this book has behind it an endless chain of those who helped. I want to express appreciation to Stephanie Egnotovich, my editor at Westminster John Knox Press, whose enthusiasm for this book from the first day to the last was a blessing. I want here to record my gratitude to my faithful assistant, Judi Harbin, whose keen eye, willing spirit, and hard work are indispensable. I want to thank the Presbyterian Church in the United States of America for the invitation to write on the first of the Great Ends of the Church."

As in all things in my life, I want to give thanks to

my past
my mother, Gladys Howell Harrington,
and my father, Jacob McLeod Harrington
my present
my wife Sara, my daughters Victoria
and Susan, and my sons-in-law, Harold and Jeff
my future
my grandchildren, Carolina,
Michael, and James

And continually, my thanks to God for the gift of life and the privilege of being a minister.

Introduction

We eagerly await the dawn of a new century! The approach of a new era holds for some, great promise, for others, great peril, and thoughtful people are trying to discern just what the new century will bring. There is a great deal of focus on the church. The 20th century began with the church proudly announcing it would be a century when the world would be claimed for Christ. All would agree, however, that we have a way to go before that becomes a reality.

A proliferation of books gives us food for thought. For example, renowned sociologist Robert Wuthnow, in his recent book *The Crises in the Churches*, describes "the spiritual malaise that has silently grown worse during the past decades." Thomas C. Reeves, professor of history at the University of Wisconsin-Parkside and Senior Fellow at the Wisconsin Policy Institute, has written a challenging book entitled *The Empty Church*. He asserts that "We should have learned by now that the religion of the golf course, the shopping mall, and the television set is no match for the moral poisons that have infected us."[1]

Allan Bloom, in *The Closing of the American Mind*, observes "The souls of young people are in a condition like that of the first men in the state of nature—spiritually unclad, unconnected, isolated, with no inherited or unconditional connection with anything or anyone. They can be anything they want to be, but they have no particular reason to want to be anything in particular."[2]

And Douglas Coupland, in his *Life After God*, has one of his characters say to his young adult friends "I know you guys think my life is some big joke—that it is going nowhere. But I'm happy. And it's not like I'm lost or anything. We're all too middle class to ever be lost. Lost means you had faith or something to begin with and the middle class never really had any of that. So we can never be lost. And you tell me, Scout, what is it we end up being, then—what exactly is it we end up being then instead of being lost?"[3]

We have come a long way from Alexis De Tocqueville's assertion that America is great because America is good. There is great concern in the American public about the quality of life in this country. The list of worries seems endless: crime, violence, drug use, pornography, divorce, illegitimate births, abortions, child abuse, poverty, teen suicides, and the breakdown of basic civility. In the ten years between 1984 and 1994, the prison population doubled to more than a million.[4] The evening news is a nightly visit to chaos and the city in which I live, love, and serve was shocked one evening to learn that a small child had choked to death on a roach in one of our public housing projects.

We are in a spiritual crisis in this nation and in the church. The church, and the people of our church, have to believe something before they can be something. The lack of spiritual focus and belief afflicts much of mainline American Protestantism. I say this with sadness. The solution to our "malaise" is found not in programs but in a return to our spiritual roots. I am not pessimistic about the future of the church because Jesus promised that the church would prevail and said that Hell's gates would not stand against it. Like many of you, I have benefited from, and been instructed by, C. S. Lewis' *The Screwtape Letters*. In the book, Lewis describes the central condition of who we are, what we are, and what we are likely to become. He describes with unmistakable clarity how the devil works to destroy the faith of a Christian: "Talk to him about 'moderation in all things.' If you can get him to the point of thinking that religion is all very well up to a point, you can feel happy about his soul. A moderate religion is as good for us as no religion at all and more amusing."

"A moderate religion" is an arresting phrase. What does it mean? It means that we profess more than we do, we talk more than we act. The Oxford historian T. R. Glover concluded that the early church advanced because it "out-thought, out-lived, and out-loved" its adversaries in the Holy Roman Empire. We must recapture that capacity because ours is a culture in which we are called upon to be the church in a world that is increasingly "unchurchly" and growing more secular with the passing of each day.

I suspect that in the church, we are dealing with an identity crisis. Who are we? The Christian faith offers us not a philosophy but instead a relationship with Jesus Christ. This relationship is then lived out in the community of faith which we call the church. The church is "the body of Christ." Our faith is not lived out in isolation, but with others. The church is the only place I know where the foundational requirement for membership is not the payment of dues but the admission of sin. I am a believer in Jesus Christ who has lived out, and is living out, my faith in the Presbyterian Church (USA). The particular church where I practice my faith is the Peachtree Presbyterian Church in Atlanta, Georgia.

Our church has defined for us who we are. We are the body of Christ who are charged with living out our faith in a particular faith within a defined framework called "The Great Ends of the Church." The Great Ends tell us who we are, what we are to do, and what business we are in. The Great Ends of the Church are:

> The proclamation of the Gospel for the salvation of humankind
>
> The shelter, nurture, and spiritual fellowship of the children of God.
>
> The maintenance of divine worship
>
> The preservation of the truth
>
> The promotion of social righteousness
>
> The exhibition of the kingdom of Heaven to the world[5]

We, as the body of Christ in the Presbyterian Church, are to proclaim, shelter and nurture, maintain divine worship, preserve the truth, promote social righteousness, and exhibit the kingdom of heaven to the world. We are to live out our faith in a world that is real, a world of need, challenge, and evil. We all have our heroes of the faith who have done all of the above and more. Their lives proclaimed the gospel and their love reached out to shelter and nourish the children of God. They were never absent from the worship of God and their lives were a testimony to truth. They modeled justice and fair play toward all, and as they walked among us, it was obvious that they marched to a distant drummer that the eye could not see and the ear could not hear, but the cadence of goodness was clear.

The cadence of goodness is clear today as well. In the church where a friend of mine was raised was a person named Dorothy. She was a permanent member of the third grade Sunday school class. Everyone in the church knew that when promoted to the third grade class, Dorothy was a member who was in charge of essential details such as handing out the pencils and checking names in the roll book. When class was over, she straightened things up and picked up the pencils. Newcomers usually thought she was the teacher's assistant. Much later, when we had grown up, we learned that Dorothy had something called Down's Syndrome. When she died in her early fifties, a long life for one with Down's Syndrome, the whole community turned out and the church was filled. No one mentioned that Dorothy had Down's Syndrome. All mentioned instead how fortunate they were to have known and loved her and how much better they were for having known her. Why? I suspect it was because they saw in her a model of the Kingdom of Heaven in the world.[6]

It is my privilege and great joy to share with you, in the pages that follow, some thoughts about the proclamation of the gospel for the salvation of humankind, the first of the Great Ends of the Church. Salvation comes by hearing and responding to the telling of the story of Jesus Christ. It is my prayer that as we make this journey together, all of us will grow to know him better and to serve him faithfully.

PART I

The Challenge

1

Proclamation is
Our Central Task

" . . . Go and make disciples in all nations."
(Matthew 28:19)

" . . . how can they believe in him if they have
never heard about him?" (Romans 10:14—*The
Living Bible*)

" . . . how welcomed are those who come
preaching God's good news!" (Romans 10:15—
The Living Bible)

Our mission is clear. There is no lack of clarity in
what our Lord has asked us, the members of the
church, to do. We are to tell the story of Jesus
Christ to those who do not believe or who have not
heard. Our mission, then, is no different than that of the
first disciples, the first believers. They were sent out to
"proclaim the gospel" and so are we. But we cannot
share with others something that we do not have. We
have to believe before we can teach. This may be the
central challenge for the church in the United States
today.

Some believe our continuing decline in mainline
America Protestantism is a crisis of belief. If we do not
believe that Jesus Christ can make a difference in our
lives and in the lives of others, why would we tell the
story? Countless individuals in the early days of our
country believed passionately that Christ made a difference in their lives. In fact, many of those who came to

these shores held on to their faith with tenacity through unbelievable hardships. They were able to do so because they believed, at the core of who and what they were, that God was with them.

Take, for example, the story of Francis Asbury. In 1771, John Wesley gave Francis Asbury the task of evangelizing the American frontier. What unfolded was one of the great achievements of our religious history. During the next thirty-two years, Asbury crisscrossed the Allegheny mountains sixty-two times.[1] He intended to be a visible presence to the hundreds of young circuit riders he recruited for ministry on the frontier. Asbury himself rode 270,000 miles and wore out at least five horses in this incredible and determined effort. In just fourteen years, by 1784, there were more than 14,000 Methodists on the frontier who were being served and shepherded in forty-two circuits.[2] The strength of his efforts, and of those who believed in the mission they were called to do, flourished long after Asbury's death in 1816. By 1844, twenty-eight years after Asbury's death, the momentum was still building. There were one million Methodists in more than 3,998 circuits with 7,730 local preachers.[3] It is easy to dismiss Asbury's effort and say "That was then, this is now." But we should not say that. The need for such an intensive effort, in our own way and in our own time, is no less than it was when Asbury faced the frontier.

There is a mission field just outside the door of all of our churches. There are people who need us and who need to hear the story of Jesus Christ. Many religious thinkers and writers today believe that at least one-half of the American population is unchurched. In fact, the Christian church in South Korea is now sending missionaries to this country.

If the mission is clear—that we are to "go and tell"— then why has the church faltered so in our time? I was ordained thirty-six years ago. Since that time, the Presbyterian Church USA has lost 35% of its membership. The losses continue unabated at the rate of more than 30,000 a year. The only area in which we have consistently grown during this period is in the number of clergy.

The Crisis

A cartoon character winds up the string on his kite. He explains to a little girl who is standing nearby, and watching with fascination, how a kite can fly. He tells her it has to do with "sail loading," the ratio of weight to surface area, and he goes on and on. She listens attentively to his rather lengthy and, I am sure, thorough explanation, and thanks him. Finally, she asks what seems to me, a basic question: "Why is the kite down the sewer?"[4] The kite was not flying, but if it had flown, it was not for long, and now it was in the "soup."

Similarly, concerning the church, we ask: if the mission is clear, then why has the church faltered so in our lifetime? I believe it is because we face a crisis of faith. For a long time we have taken the Christian faith for granted in our society. Our churches are plentiful and many of them have been in place in communities across this land for generations. Why all the fuss? The fuss is because we are in massive decline and the alternative to growth is death.

We have an urgent need to renew our capacity to "proclaim the gospel for the salvation of humankind." Several issues dominate now. The community of faith that we all love is divided and our debates are characterized by acrimony. What kind of spirit does it represent when, at the highest level of our church, one church person refers to those who disagree as "theological terrorists?" At worst, it is a poor witness to the world of how Christians are not loving one another as our Lord commanded. At best, it is what my mother would call "bad manners."

We cannot merely dismiss the plight of our church as being a part of the climate of the time. Martin Luther King, Jr., used a wonderful metaphor in *Letter from Birmingham City Jail*: "We are to be more than theological thermometers just measuring the temperature of our time. We are, instead, to be thermostats, setting the temperature of our time. Our impact is lessened and our proclamation is timid and tepid precisely because we are more "blenders" than "proclaimers." Have we forgotten that we are not to be conformed to this world, but to be transformed in Christ? It is our loss of inner direction that allows the world around us to crush us into its mold."

It may well be that the church has been preoccupied with too many issues instead of focused on the central issue of proclamation. Is it possible that because we have been more concerned about preserving our "structures" we have lost sight of our redemptive purpose? What the church offers to the world is a relationship to Jesus Christ; that relationship is lived out in a community of faith—the church—which is called "the body of Christ." It is this community of faith that is to be the "Christ" to the nation and the world. We are to be Jesus' hands, to feed the hungry and house the homeless; the feet to nurture the sick and those who mourn, and to visit the prisoners; the eyes to seek out the lost who need to be found by the Christ who loves them; and the ears to hear the cries of need that rise endlessly.

It is not going to be easy. No one promised that it would be. Our task begins with the proclamation of the good news of one who came that "we might have life and have it more abundantly." The proclamation is to be done in a world that is increasingly secular, where often when the essential decisions of life—marriage, family, education, vocation, and morality—are made, God is left out. And it is to be done in a world where "designer religion" is popular. It is called "new age." One adds a little of this and a little of that, and a new religion is created. It is the gently packaged heresy of our time. It makes few demands and delivers very little when the chips are down. Subjective religion cannot stand the tests of either time or life. Like the golden calf in the wilderness, it is good to dance around but of little use for anything else.

The other day a young woman said to me "I have faith in myself and little else." What happens when she loses faith in herself? There will come a day when self-confidence is not enough. In recent months, I have dealt with more tragedy and loss than during any other comparable period of my ministry. Where would you be without faith when crib death takes a three-month-old child? Where would you be without faith when you are told at age forty-four you have terminal cancer and the outer limits of your life are about three to six months? Where would you be without faith if both you and your spouse were struggling with terminal lung cancer and your son had a melanoma removed from his back?

Searching

On the other side of our mobile, chaotic, violent society is a tremendous searching, a kind of desperate search. People have "been there and done that," and they hunger for something more. When they come to my study for a visit, they express this hunger in a variety of ways: "Something is missing in my life and I cannot figure out what it is;" "I want my life to count for something more than selling stocks and managing portfolios;" or "It suddenly dawned on me that I can't figure out what I would be remembered for if I were to die." St. Augustine wrote that our hearts are "restless till they find their rest in Thee." It is that transcendent connection that is missing. The heart longs for that connectedness.

In recent Fourth of July celebrations, I noted something that I read about Thomas Jefferson. He is buried in the family cemetery on the grounds of his home, Monticello, just outside of Charlottesville, Virginia. This inscription on his tomb fascinated me: "Here is buried Thomas Jefferson, author of the Declaration of American Independence, Statute of Virginia for Religious Freedom, and Father of The University of Virginia."

It struck me suddenly that many things were left out. There was no mention of his serving as Governor of Virginia, member of Congress, Ambassador to France, Secretary of State, Vice President of the United States, or President of the United States. I suspect the reason is that Thomas Jefferson wrote his own epitaph. He wanted most to be remembered for his love of freedom. He had given himself passionately to a cause that was far larger than he. It is this larger cause, this spiritual centering, that is missing in many of us and I believe it is what we are seeking. We experience, in the church which I serve, hundreds of earnest seekers.

They come seeking some certainties larger than what they feel, touch, taste, handle, and see. There is a spiritual hunger around us that sets the scene for our renewal and recovery as a church. Renewal is dependent on our focus in the "proclamation of the gospel for the salvation of humankind."

The eager seekers hear and understand our proclamation by what we say, by who we are, and by how we serve. A belief has developed, and I think it is increasing, that the proclaiming is done exclusively by the clergy. But as I recall, there were no ordained persons in the disciple band around Jesus. The whole issue of ordination came much later in the church. All of us, clergy and laity, are to be proclaimers. We have let others define "evangelism" for us in ways that make us uncomfortable. We are not to "assault one who may not believe" but are to tell the story of Jesus and his love. Theologian Reinhold Niebuhr said we are "to charm people into righteousness." The simple witness of our life and the sharing of what Christ has meant to us is proclamation. D. T. Niles said that evangelism is "one beggar telling another where to find some bread." All of us have a unique story to tell, and we must tell it because Christ commanded us to "go" and to "tell."

Marilyn Monroe has become a cultural "icon." I suspect this has to do with the tragic way in which she died. Unbeknownst to many on the night she died, she turned on a tape machine that recorded the last hours of her life. A young reporter discovered the original tape and was puzzled by what he heard. In the closing moments of her life, Marilyn Monroe had cried out again and again, "Tony, Tony, Oh Tony, where are you?" No one knew who "Tony" was. The reporter continued to search for the answer but it seemed to be a dead end. Finally, he made his way to a recording shop where Marilyn Monroe worked before she became a star. He talked to a clerk who had worked with her, and during the interview the clerk responded to a question with "Tony would have liked that!" The reporter was shocked and said that for more than a year he had been looking for a person named "Tony" who apparently knew Marilyn Monroe. The reporter asked "Who is Tony?" He learned that "Tony" had been Marilyn Monroe's nickname for many years. Her death takes on a new meaning with this information. As the end drew near, she called for "Tony," asking "Where are you?" She died, as many do, looking for herself.[5]

I can tell you that the "fields are white unto the harvest." We are in a challenging time, but it is a time for proclaimers to step forward and tell the story. Those who are searching for themselves need to hear the story that only we can tell.

For Reflection and Discussion

1. How central is the "centrality of proclamation" in the church you attend? Are the "members" of the church involved, or is it assumed that "proclamation" is the task of the clergy?

2. Are people in your church encouraged to tell the story of their faith journey? As D. T. Niles said, "It is one beggar telling another where to find some bread."

3. Do you believe that the mission field is "just outside the door of all of our churches?"

4. How are you, personally, proclaiming the gospel to this mission field? How is your church accomplishing this mission?

5. What does your relationship to Jesus Christ mean to you? How do you tell others about that relationship?

2

We Proclaim Because Sinners Need a Savior

"It seems to be a fact of life that when I want to do right, I inevitably do wrong." (Romans 7:21—*The Living Bible*)

" . . . all have sinned and fallen short of the glory of God." (Romans 3:23—*New King James Version*)

" . . . while we were still sinners, Christ died for us." (Romans 5:8—*New King James Version*)

We all know that we are not measuring up, but we do make excuses; and more and more, we make light of missing the mark. Ortega y Gassett wrote about people who have grown tired of being ordered and commanded and who now with "holiday air take advantage of a period freed from burdensome imperatives." We are not free from the imperatives of right living: we are just acting that way. We still lie awake at night and weep for our sins.

When we are freed from "imperatives," even in our own minds, then the result is what William Butler Yeats described in "The Second Coming"

. . . things fall apart; the centre cannot hold; Mere anarchy is loosed upon the world, the blood-dimmed tide is loosed, and everywhere the ceremony of innocence is drowned; The best lack all conviction, while the worst are full of passionate intensity.

Karl Menninger wrote a landmark book more than two decades ago entitled *What Ever Became of Sin*. In the opening scene, an intense man is pursuing a ministry of sorts at a busy intersection in the city of Chicago. It turns out to be an effective ministry. He suddenly confronts a pedestrian making his way to some destination and shouts in his face: "Guilty!" One would expect that such a confrontation would result in anger, but to the contrary, the person who was confronted with the verdict of "guilty" from a stranger dropped his head as if in deep thought, and moved on down the street. I suspect that in a moment of "reality therapy," they were both suddenly aware that the verdict was true. We are all guilty of sin and the Bible articulates this with unmistakable clarity: " . . . all have sinned and fallen short of the glory of God." (Romans 3:23)

We are all against sin and sometimes are aghast at what we see in our time. New words have emerged in our vocabularies such as "drive-by shootings" and "car jackings." Brutality and violence are commonplace and our children listen to rap songs that call for the killing of policemen or the sexual mutilation of women. But there is an additional sin: the overwhelming evidence of aberrant behavior and the brutal display of sin today cause us to simply "lament for a moment and then become accustomed to it." Senator Daniel Patrick Moynihan calls this "defining deviancy downward." Sin is much with us. Who can doubt it? We know the problem; but what is the solution?

There is no "self-help" program that can or will serve as a remedy for the reality of sin. The only remedy for sinners is a savior. How will those who are burdened by their sins know about a savior unless we proclaim the reality of one? If a poll was taken today in our churches, I suspect you would find that we are all against sin. Our statements about the challenge of sin would be as autobiographic as those of the Apostle Paul when he wrote in the book of Romans: "What I want to do, I do not" (7:15), "What I don't want to do, I do" (7:15), "I know perfectly well the difference between right and wrong" (7:16), "I suffer agony of conscience because I have done wrong" (7:16), and "My propensity for sin is stronger than my desire to do what is right" (7:16).

I cannot speak for you but I can speak for myself. Those statements resonate as truth in my own life. There is a constant tension in each of our lives between what God would have us be and what we in fact are. Paul went so far as to call himself "the chief of sinners."

We know the predicament of the reality of sin in our own lives, but what is the remedy? Paul knew the answer and shared it with us: "Thank God! It has been done by Jesus Christ, our Lord. He has set me free" (Romans 7:25). Christ is the answer. It is grace that we need and it is grace that comes with the proclamation of the gospel. Pastor Leonard Sweet challenges the church and its members: "Postmodern culture has a moral atmosphere of zero. In a zero-morality culture, the church must pump up the atmosphere with the gravity of grace.[1]

We proclaim the gospel for the salvation of humankind. Sinners need a savior. Look at the proliferation of self-help books that are almost without number. But the remedy for sin is not found in something that we can do for ourselves. We can buy into "positive thinking," we can practice all of the "be happy attitudes," and we can be "possibility thinkers," all of which can be helpful to us. But the reality of sin must be faced. We can point at the systemic evil around and about us but sooner or later, we have to face the banquet of consequences that is ours and ours alone.

The Bible uses words and phrases to describe sin and instruct us such as "missing the mark," "straying from the fold," or "journeying into a far country." "Sin" is the insistence on doing things "my way." We all know that "our way" is not always God's way. We all try to avoid the reality or the responsibility for our sins. Landon Gilkey, who wrote *Shantung Compound*, described his World War II prisoner-of-war experience in a Japanese concentration camp in China. During that time, he had ample opportunity to observe human behavior. He came to this conclusion about sin:

> Sin may be defined as an ultimate religious devotion to a finite interest; it is an overriding loyalty of concern for the self, its existence and its

prestige . . . from this inordinate love of the self and its own, stem the moral evils of indifference, injustice, prejudice and cruelty to one's neighbor, and the other destructive patterns of action we call "sin."[2]

Any way you cut it, we are responsible for our sins. When we do wrong, it is against the wishes of God. It often hurts others, and it always hurts us by creating an estrangement between us and God. David Myers, a keen student of human behavior, identifies three characteristics that reveal the foundations of our flawed and sinful behavior.

First, we display a "self-serving bias." We take more ownership of our successes than we do our failures. In a study, researchers gave willing participants some tests. When the tests were over, some participants were told they had failed, others that they had succeeded. Those who succeeded acknowledged they had always been superior in the field tested. Those who failed attributed it to "rotten luck." They said they were just having a bad day and, frankly, knew the material well. The pattern is clear. "I succeeded because of my ability" and "I failed because some unknown reason caused me to fail."

Second, we are "biased favorably in any self-assessment." When assessment times come, we are in favor of ourselves. Drivers who have been hospitalized because of a severe traffic accident describe themselves as better-than-average drivers when it comes to safety. An educational testing service asked one million high school seniors to rate themselves with their peers. Sixty percent said that, all modesty aside, they were better. Only six percent said they were worse. In the "ability to get along with others" category, zero percent rated themselves below average.

Third, we "overestimate the goodness of our actions." We exaggerate our virtues and minimize our vices. In Indiana, 60 percent of people asked said they would be glad to help in volunteer efforts for the Cancer Fund. When the time came to volunteer, only four percent volunteered. We have all experienced that, haven't we!

Have you tried to recruit volunteers for Sunday School of late? Many indicated that they would volunteer, but it was difficult getting them there on a given Sunday.[3]

The truth is often far different from our promises. Many of our promises are hollow and many of our words are empty. Even when our promises are strong, our follow-through is weak. This is the human condition. David Myers' observations imply that we are suffering from a "superiority complex," or the sin of pride. Pride, you will recall, is the first of the Seven Deadly Sins. The Bible has a comprehensive view of us all at the point of sin: " . . . for all have sinned and fall short of the glory of God" (Romans 3:23).

We are sinners in need of a savior and in need of grace. There is no way out of this dilemma until we acknowledge our need for the grace of God.

As Christians, if we are not careful, we sometimes assume that once we have made a profession of faith, the personal "civil war" is over inside. In fact, we will struggle all of our lives over what we want as opposed to what God wills for our lives. Our human "will" always wants to embrace what God abhors. Several years ago, for example, former President Jimmy Carter spoke from the pulpit of Peachtree Presbyterian Church. He talked to us about sacrifice. He told us how good he felt about his Christian witness. In fact, he acknowledged that he was downright proud of his witness for Christ. By his own account, he had led 140 persons to a decision about Jesus Christ. As that moving thought sank in a bit, the former president, in a moment of refreshing candor, said that upon reflection, he did not feel quite so proud about it. He recalled the human effort he had made to be elected governor of Georgia in a rather exhausting campaign. In the course of that effort, he had shaken hands personally with 600,000 Georgians and asked them if they would vote for him on election day. He then realized, as we all do at some point, that his efforts for Christ were minimal compared to his exertions in response to self-interest.

Christians will struggle with sin for as long as they live. The only way they will ever make it is through grace. Paul knew he did not have the capacity to extract himself from the dilemma of sin, so he asked "Who will free me?" Only Christ can set us free. He has made provision for our freedom and we need to accept his grace.

There is a prison in the city of Sao Dos Campos, Brazil. It was turned over to two Christians twenty years ago. It is called Humanita and is run according to Christian principles. The prison has only two full-time people on staff. The rest of the work is done by the inmates. Every prisoner has a partner to whom he or she is accountable. Every prisoner goes to Chapel or takes a course in character formation. Every prisoner is assigned to a volunteer family outside of the prison who becomes part of that prisoner's life while in prison and this family makes the prisoner a part of their lives. This relationship continues when the prisoner is finally released.

Charles Colson of Prison Fellowship visited the prison some time ago. When he arrived, he found that the prisoners who greeted him were smiling. Their living areas were clean and the walls were covered with verses from the Bible. The recidivism rate there is four % as opposed to the average 75% in a regular Brazilian or American prison. What is the secret? A guide took Colson to what served at one time as the isolation cell. The man who took him there was serving time for murder. The cell was once the ultimate maximum punishment for incorrigibles. When they got to the door of the cell, the prisoner asked Colson "Are you sure you want to go in?" Colson said "yes," and the massive door swung open. Both of them looked at the "prisoner" in that isolation cell. There was a crucifix, beautifully carved by the prison inmates of the prisoner Jesus hanging on the cross. The guide, in a whisper, said "He's doing time for all the rest of us!"[4]

It is that story that we must proclaim to all who will listen. All who hear our proclamation are sinners in need of a savior.

For Reflection and Discussion

1. What would happen if you asked ten of your closest friends to list the Ten Commandments?

2. Do you really believe that sinners are lost without a savior? What does that mean to your faith?

3. Do you believe that sin at is foundation is selfishness?

4. Do you believe the church is relevant to your life? How? Why or why not?

5. President Jimmy Carter reflected that his efforts for Christ were minimal by comparison to his exertions in response to self-interest. In what ways have you proclaimed the gospel for Christ? In what ways could you do more?

6. We "all sin and fall short of the glory of God." As Christians, we know that Christ died for us and through the gift of grace offers us hope. How do we share that knowledge with others? What specifically can we do differently to proclaim the gospel of salvation to our world?

7. In a private moment, reflect on what the five most pressing temptations of your life are. Then think what you are going to do, with God's help, about them.

3

If Your Church Ceased to Exist, Would Anyone Miss it?

" . . . What do ye, more than others?" (Matthew 5:47)

I participated recently in a gathering of ministers from across denominational lines. It was a diverse group and we brainstormed together about the challenges the church faces as we move into the Twenty-first Century. We identified two important challenges:

1. The challenge of being called upon to minister to a society that is "unchurched" and increasingly secular. This reality represents our hidden opportunity if we grasp it. Research routinely asserts that unchurched people are engaged in religious activity. Forty to sixty percent report praying to God. Thirty to forty percent report reading the Bible regularly. Seventy to eighty percent say faith and religion are important in their lives.[1]

2. The challenge of reaching hundreds of young people who are earnestly "seeking after" spiritual things. Many of them are the children of "boomers" (30 million of whom have not participated in the church). It is my great privilege to serve a church in which we have 3,500 members who are under the age of thirty-five. We are on the cutting edge of responding to the spiritual needs of many who are experiencing church for the first time with us. This genera-

tion represents a great opportunity for us if we grasp it. It is this promise that has caused George G. Hunter, III to assert: "The Christian movement now faces its greatest opportunity in the Western world in the last three centuries."[2]

The high moment of the conference came for me when our leader raised a sobering question: "If the church you currently serve ceased to exist, who would miss it? Would anyone notice or care that it was gone?"

It was an unthinkable thought and one that I immediately personalized. I cannot imagine that the grand church which I have served now as pastor for nearly twenty-seven years could cease to exist. It is unthinkable that seventy-nine years of work and sacrifice would be lost. If it happened, how could any of us face those who came before us and bore the burden of strong witness for Christ through wars and depression? As I turned the question over in my mind, I began to refine it a bit and asked a companion inquiry: If Peachtree Presbyterian Church at 3434 Roswell Road, NW, Atlanta, Georgia, ceased to exist, would the current members of the church miss it?

You have heard that often repeated warning that "the church is just one generation from extinction." We have heard it, but we do not believe it, do we? Robert Frost, who lived into his nineties, once said that one of the most basic things he had learned about life was that "life goes on."

Honesty requires me to admit that some of our members would not miss it because they are rarely in attendance. They sit on the sidelines, infrequent spectators at best, nonparticipants most of the time. Some of our unidentified visitors, who have come for years but never made a commitment to membership, would not miss Peachtree Presbyterian. I suspect they would soon drift to another church and become unidentified there. I rather suspect that it is the "barely good" who cause churches to die and cease to exist.

I know that the CHURCH, in capital letters, will endure. Jesus promised that it would. He said that the "gates of Hell would not prevail against it." He did not promise that any particular church would endure. There is no guarantee that it will. Each generation has to pass the torch to another. Each generation must build with strength on the foundation and heritage that it has been given. We all know of churches that ceased to exist as churches. The buildings still stand, but it is now a restaurant, or in one case, a garage where cars are repaired. I have seen these "dead" churches all over England and Scotland and in New England, where many are now town halls or arenas for flea markets and art festivals.

If the church where you are currently a member ceased to exist, who would miss it? This is a searching question! Thousands of religious orders of one kind or another were established and functioned for a time in Christian history, but only eighteen remain. And only two of the eighteen that remain are viable. What sets us apart? What makes us different, unique, indispensable, or so essential that we would be missed if we no longer existed? The theme verse which began this chapter asks the essential question: "What do ye, more than others?" (Matthew 5:47)

In response to this, I want to pose a question of my own. Is your church a force or a fixture? Webster defined fixture as "a state of being fixed," in blunt terms and not subject to change. Many churches are in this condition even though things all about us are changing constantly. If our churches are to become a force, many of them will have to change. The issue before us is how churches formed in a "churched" society adapt to the challenges in what is now an "unchurched" society.

Ironically, one of the things about which the church concerns itself is change. When the gospel is proclaimed, things change. Men and women are "made new" in Christ. We have many expressions that indicate this reality. We say that John has "walked from darkness into light." That represents change. We asked a friend if she had heard that Mary experienced "conversion?" Conversion means change. Basic to the mission of the church is change, and Peter Drucker has said that " . . . any organization that forgets its mission dies."[3]

Declining Churches: The Telltale Signs

The church you attend will cease being an effective force it it is in decline. Declining churches become preoccupied with survival. As a result, they focus inward on themselves and do little outreach in terms of mission or people. Alan C. Klaas, in his thought-provoking book *In Search of the Unchurched*, says that declining churches share seven characteristics.

1. Members have a "poor me" attitude about their congregation. Basically, they do not believe in themselves or their mission. They are often apologetic about their church and use terms like "We are small," "We are struggling," or "We can barely keep the doors open." Meetings of their governing board almost always begin with a discussion of financial problems. Meetings focus not on potential but on problems. The focus is consistently internal. Because there are no dreams for reaching out or claiming new opportunities, the feel of decline is everywhere.

2. Members are not aware of their congregation's strengths. How could they be aware of any areas of strength when their total focus is on the reasons why they are not strong? They are so problem-oriented that they never notice opportunity so it is not a part of their conversation. If the focus changed to "potential," they could create some positive experiences in the church.

    In the early months of my service as pastor of Peachtree Presbyterian, I realized that we needed to lift the morale of the congregation. The members did not expect great things to happen. The first opportunity we had to do something different was at the annual world mission offering. The previous year, the offering had amounted to about $2,500.00. We decided we would raise money to send a tractor to our mission in Zaire. No one believed that it could be done. But early one cold Sunday morning in February 1972, an Elder drove a tractor down Roswell Road and parked it on the front steps of the church. No one could get into the church for several Sundays without walking around that tractor. The effect was electrifying. We raised all that was needed and more! Even more important, a positive "can do" spirit swept through the congregation.

3. Members are not involved in their congregation's neighborhood. The church is an island of isolation, surrounded by the neighborhood. The neighbors do not bother us; we do not bother them.

    At one time, the facilities of Peachtree Presbyterian were like this, locked up during the week and open only on Sunday. Today, it is very different. The buildings are used by 15,000 people every week and on four nights during the week, every room in the building is in use. In fact, our weekday Bible studies are growing faster than our Sunday School program. Ironically, during one of our requests for zoning before the City Council of Atlanta, the group that opposed our zoning met weekly in our facilities. Your church can be opened to community activities as well.

4. The congregation is served by a few, long-term lay leaders. The leadership question is tricky. There are two basic issues: first, we should always be developing the next generation of leaders. Leadership structures that become a closed circle inevitably become wed to strategies of "former glories." Second, no matter how fine the existing leaders are they can "burn out." When this happens, nothing positive will occur in the life of the church. Leaders will respond to new ideas with catch phrases such as "We don't do things that way

here," "We have never done it that way before," "We tried that here several years ago and it did not work," or "You don't really understand this church, do you?" The new member gets the message: "New ideas are not going to be considered here."

5. The community around the church is declining. This becomes a self-fulfilling prophecy: if the community is declining, it is reasonable to expect that the church will decline as well. I can show you church after church that became the agent of change that not only turned the church around with its creative outreach, but also turned the community around as well. These congregations and their leadership did not sit around helplessly and let the church die along with the community.

6. The congregation sets up invisible barriers. We set up these barriers without thinking about what we are doing. For example, we keep the church locked up all week or we don't greet people on Sunday. We might advertise ourselves as "The Church of the Open Door" but don't you believe it. Any church can become an inviting fellowship. The reality is that the best evangelism is invitational. Andrew, the Disciple, always invited people to come with him to meet Jesus. If your church is invitational, it will grow because people will sense the genuineness of your invitation and feel welcome.

   Stop looking for some gimmick to cause your church to grow. The best and most natural way is to get your members talking about what is happening and what is going to happen at your church. Although the Peachtree Presbyterian Church has televised its services for twenty-five years, approximately 70% of those who visit our church first learned about it by word of mouth. For example, a member of the congregation told a friend what was happening; a co-worker in a member's office was invited to a program; and a family invited a next-door neighbor to the annual church picnic. If you become an inviting congregation, many of the "invisible barriers" will come down.

7. Declining congregations see themselves as a family. On the surface, this might seem to be good, but it is not. It excludes people and ideas. If you are not in the family, forget it. Remember how people become a family. They marry into it or they are born into it. If we are not careful, the concept of "family" can become a closed system and nonfamily members will not feel welcome![4]

Is your church a fixture or a force? It is a basic question. Fixtures do not change, but there is nothing as predictable as change. Things that do not change inevitably decline and die. Churches that are vital and growing are always changing. Webster defines "force" in many ways but hits the nail on the head when he says that force is "to press, drive, attain, or effect against resistance or inertia." A church that is a force for God and for good is always moving and reaching out. The late Leslie Newbigin described the faithful church and what it will be: "the church that is a force for God will be a community of praise . . . a community of truth . . . a community that does not live for itself . . . a community where men and women are prepared for and are sustained in the exercise of their priesthood of believers in the world . . . a communion of mutual responsibility . . . a community of hope."[5]

If your church is a force, all of this, and more, is present. If not, take a close look at what needs to be done to enhance the proclamation of the gospel. The chapel at Belmont Abbey College contains a striking baptismal font. The font is hollowed out of a huge piece of granite. When you look at it, your eyes are drawn to a plaque which reads "On this rock, slaves were once traded and sold. From this rock, people are now baptized and set free in Christ."[6]

That statement is a challenge to every church that things need not stay the same. We are called, in Christ, to be all that we can be for him.

Another point in response to the question of "what do ye, more than others?" is what would happen if your church ceased to exist? This is a question of evaluation. Are we doing anything that would be lost if we no longer existed? It is a good exercise to think of the unthinkable from time to time. Think about your church and the following scenarios.

You have served a farming area for generations. The church was once the center of the community, both socially and spiritually. Then the children married and moved away. They come home for occasional visits and the annual homecoming but yours is now the smallest of the churches in a five-church field. Your membership is down to about thirty, and the average age of your congregation is seventy-five. Your services are only held twice a month and the pastor lives forty miles away. Homecoming this past year drew only a handful of relatives who came home for the event. The handwriting is on the wall: this church is dying. What can be done?

For years, your church was solid in a community that is now a growing metropolitan area. The urban environment changed, the neighborhood changed, the area is becoming commercialized, and a developer wants to buy your property. The Presbytery thinks it is a good idea because they could use the money from the sale for "new church development." The church in which your grandparents were charter members, your parents met and married, you were baptized as a child, and were married is going to disappear. One day soon, you will drive by the site and see a shopping center.

Who would miss It? The world will pass by the shopping center every day. Unless someone tells them a church was there for one-hundred years, they will never know that here vows were said and prayers uttered, good-byes were said to loved ones, and the laughter of children at Bible School was heard. All of those voices are silent, and no one misses them. Perhaps the church would have made it if it had been more responsive to changes and encroaching commercial development. Perhaps the people were no longer committed to its life and the proclamation of the gospel was just for those who were there and not for those who were passing by or passing through.

The Death of a Church: the Consequences

The death of any church anywhere is never inconsequential. When it happens, there are three consequences:

1. The search for the sacred in that place is diminished. The church at the seat of the county, the church in the center of a large farming region, or the church on a busy city street is symbolic of the presence of God in that place. But more than that, it is the home of a community of faith searching for a deeper current in their lives. The church responds to our spiritual needs and pointing us faithfully toward God. Where the Gospel is being proclaimed, there is the constant challenge for us to walk in the footsteps of Christ.

   I think about this reality every time I stand to preach. There are always visitors present. In a city church, you preach to a "passing parade." There are persons present each Sunday who will never be there again. Some are in the city for the weekend, just passing through; others are there because a friend's baby is being baptized and who will return to their home community after the service. However, the message should be clear to all who come. They should experience the presence of God; they should hear the gospel proclaimed; they should be challenged to reach higher and to live with a sense of Christlike purpose.

We are missing one of the operative elements in many of our churches by not appealing to the heroic dimension that God placed in us. We offer "bargain basement" faith which Wilbur Rees described: "I would like to buy $3.00 worth of God, please. Not enough to disturb my soul or to keep me awake. Just enough to equal a cup of warm milk, or a snooze in the sunshine. I don't want enough of God to make me love a person of another race, or pick beets with a migrant worker. I want ecstasy and not transformation. I want the warmth of the womb, but not a new birth. I want a pound of eternity in a paper bag. I would like to buy just $3.00 worth of God, if you please."[7]

A church probably *should* go out of existence if it is not preaching and living in response to a gospel that seeks to transform. The churches that call for an ever-deepening commitment to Christ are generally thriving. A church that reluctantly calls, or urges, a minimal response will not make much of a mark. Certainly, we should preach the God of all comfort, but we should not preach "Do as you please, and be comfortable." We certainly remind our members that God is a "present help in time of trouble," but we should urge our members to stay out of trouble. The church should be the conscience of the community, challenging unworthy behavior, and calling for an ever-deepening commitment to Christ. A deep commitment to Christ will challenge our prejudices and move us in life and witness out to places we have never been before.

2. A second consequence of the death of a church is that the search for the least, the lowest, and the lost is diminished. We take so much for granted. We think the church is indestructible. The church has always been there;

it will always be there. Church is "God's thing," and God will always provide for the church. But in reality, the church exists on earth to do the work of God. Your church exists for better or for worse; it is what the people want it to be. It should be looking outward so that those who are on the raw edge of human need will feel its support and caring. Who would have gone into Techwood Homes in Atlanta, the oldest public housing project in America, if Peachtree Presbyterian had not gone? No one else *had* gone. You have the equivalent of that challenge wherever you live. It is in places of darkness and need that we become, in reality, as our lives touch others, the light of the world and the salt of the earth.

Habitat for Humanity has a simple mission statement: "Everyone on earth shall have a simple decent home." To even think such a thought is madness! However, in pursuit of that powerful dream, Habitat for Humanity is now the sixteenth largest homebuilder in America.[8] Habitat has built more than 61,000 homes in more than fifty countries around the world and is currently building about 10,000 to 12,000 houses a year. Why? Because Jesus Christ sent us to build homes for the homeless. And Habitat's primary funding base is the church.

Wherever the gospel is proclaimed for the salvation of humankind, people reach out to those who need them such as the desperate and the lost. If your church has never built a home with Habitat, it should. If we could get the 300,000 churches in America to build just one house, we could impact the challenge of homelessness in America in a dramatic fashion. Some years ago, the Governor of Mississippi, Kirk Fordice, issued a challenge to the 5,500 churches and synagogues in his state to adopt just one poor person and help that person get back on his or her feet. Two hundred and sixty-seven of the 5,500 churches and synagogues took up the challenge. As of late 1996, only fifteen of the 5,500 churches and synagogues were still matched up with a person.[9]

3. A third consequence of the death of church is that our reach for excellence for the glory of God would be diminished. The Bible teaches us that we are to give God the "first fruits," not the leftovers. The church of Jesus Christ is: " . . . where you send what is at the bottom of the barrel instead of the 'cream of the crop'."

God has given us much to work with, presented challenging opportunities for us to meet, and requests our best in response to these blessings. We should encourage in each other our best for God. I recently read a story about a remarkable teacher. The story is entitled *The Whisper Test* and was written by Mary Ann Bird. Mary Ann had some physical disabilities that caused her classmates to ask "What happened to you?" Their questions and stares caused her much pain and as a result, she came to expect little love outside of her own family.

When Mary Ann reached the second grade, she learned that her teacher, Mrs. Leonard, was a very popular teacher. As the school year began, Mrs. Leonard gave all the second graders a hearing test. Mary Ann dreaded the test because she was virtually deaf in one ear. She watched as the students stood by the door and covered one ear. Mrs. Leonard, seated nearby, would whisper something from a few feet away; "The sky is blue" or "Do you have new shoes?" The children would then repeat what she had said.

When Mary Ann's turn came for the test, she heard seven words that changed her life: "I wish you were my little girl!" When her teacher said those words, Mary Ann Bird affirmed that God must have been speaking through Mrs. Leonard. When we proclaim the gospel of Jesus Christ, one of the messages that comes through is that God loves us and expects us to love one another. God looks down at all of our imperfections and disabilities and says: "I know that you are not perfect, but I love you anyway, and I want you to be my child."[10]

The church exists to tell the story and to live the story. If we tell it effectively, we will become motivated and will motivate others to give their best.

It is unthinkable to contemplate that the church in the particular place that we live could cease to exist: the church that nourished us, shaped us, and wept with us. Then challenges came and we felt the strength of its fellowship. It is unthinkable. Can it really happen? The answer is, yes, it can! A particular church in a particular place can cease to exist. Ask yourself this fundamental question: If every member of the church where I am a member supported the church as I do, would it endure, or would it cease to exist?

What becomes of particular churches depends on the particular members of that church. Someone recently sent me a cartoon. I do not know where it came from or who developed it. A clergyperson stands at the door of a church. The service is over and a crowd of decidedly happy people are crowded around him. One man says "Are we glad to hear that you don't know where you'll get the money you need—for a minute there we were afraid you wanted to get it from us!"

The future of our church may depend on you. Are you dependable?

For Reflection and Discussion

1. Do you take your church, its life, and its mission for granted?

2. If we are the "light of the world" why is it so dark in so many places?

3. If we are the "salt of the earth" why is the "flavor" of who and what we are supposed to be as Christians so bland?

4. Do you agree that in the midst of change some things remain the same such as the hunger of the human heart for God, the desire for meaning, and the need to make a difference?

5. Is your church open and inviting during the week or is it closed? Are you happy about that?

6. How inviting is your church? List the ways in which you see your church and its people as invitational.

7. Do you appoint "greeters" or do you ask the entire congregation to be open and responsive to visitors?

8. List the things that would be lost if the church where you are now a member ceased to exist.

9. If you were arrested for being a Christian, would there be enough evidence to convict you?

10. Would anyone notice or care if your church ceased to exist? Would you miss it? In what ways?

11. What is the morale of your congregation?

12. How does your church measure up with the criteria of declining churches? Are there areas you need to examine or changes that need to be made?

13. Does your church ask for a deepening, life-changing commitment to Christ? Have you experienced that in your own life?

14. "The church exists to tell the story and to live the story." List ways your church is doing these two things. If you aren't satisfied with your list, what are some changes you could make to accomplish these things?

4

The Church's Survival in America

"Where two or three are gathered in my name, I am there among them." (Matthew 18:20)

"Christ the head of the Church, which is his body." (Ephesians 1:22–23)

Will Durant, in his book *The Story of Civilization*, pays great tribute to the church. He writes:

"There is no greater drama in human history on record than the sight of a few Christians, scorned and oppressed by a succession of emperors, bearing all trials with fierce tenacity, muyltiplying quietly, building order while their enemies generate chaos, fighting sword with the word of God, brutality with hope, and at least defeating the strongest state that history has known. Caesar and Christ had met, and Christ won."[1]

Durant wrote in tribute to the endurance, the tenacity, and the faithfulness of the church to its mission, a faithfulness lived in the face of persecution.

We in America tend to take the church for granted. As I have said before in this book, we are called upon today to proclaim the gospel in an unchurched society. George G. Hunter, III, advocates a new lifestyle for the church as we meet both the challenge and opportunity of our time. He urges us to acknowledge that . . .

We are called to *live* in the world but *not* of it. That is, we are called to live by a different set of values than the world lives by.

We are called to a life of service and ministry, echoing John Wesley's belief that the church ought to do "good to all people."

We are called to a life of witness and mission. The mission is holistic in that it cares for the body, the physical needs of people, and for the soul as we nurture the inner life.

In Jesus Christ we discover our identity. We are the "body of Christ" in this world.[2]

One of the greatest challenges the church faces in any age is the burden of the imperfection of its members, members who are indifferent, apathetic, and who often profess more faith than they practice. Walk into any church in America and sit quietly and look around. The people you see are not perfect. At the heart of each is a flaw, a failure, something broken, sometimes too broken to be mended. Yet the church endures and will endure. I believe in the years just ahead of us, the church is going to thrive again in America and some believe we are already in the early stages of a new religious awakening.

The late columnist Lewis Grizzard said he was "an American by birth and a Southerner by the grace of God." Lewis said that he witnessed his first miracle in the Moreland United Methodist Church in Moreland, georgia. It was the church of his childhood and remained his church until he died. Two Moreland boys had gotten into trouble and had been sentenced by the authorities to attend the youth group at Moreland United Methodist for six months. Perfect attendance was mandated. Lewis was present when they showed up for the first time at the youth group. The first night there they beat up two other boys in the group and threw a hymn book at the kindly lady who was the group's leader. She adroitly ducked the book and said to the two boys, "I don't approve of what you boys did here tonight, and neither does Jesus Christ. But if he can forgive you, I guess I can."

Then she passed a plate of cookies she had baked for the group to the two boys and invited them to help themselves. Years later, when Grizzard was attending services at the church one Sunday, he learned that the two boys had grown up to be good fathers, held steady jobs, and rarely if ever missed church. Lewis concluded his column by saying, "It was the first miracle I ever saw!"[3]

The church is a miracle. There are some 300,000 churches in this country. We often ignore them, heap scorn upon them, or accuse them of being irrelevant and out of touch. All of that is sometimes true but what would we do without the church? If all of the churches we have known, loved, and counted on in trying times were suddenly removed, what would happen? I believe the country would grind to a halt in a short time. Who would pick up the slack of comfort not given, conflicts not resolved, trouble not listened to? And who would absorb the stresses and strains of the human condition that the church routinely absorbs? The church offers a loving heart and a listening ear in a noisy and indifferent world.

The Church as the Body of Christ

The church lives out its life with many assuring promises. None of those promises is more precious than the one written in Matthew 18:20 which states " . . . where two or three are gathered in my name, I am there among them."

Nor are they more precious than the way Paul, when writing to the Christians in Ephesus, described who we are as the church: " . . . Christ the head of the Church, which is His body." (Ephesians 1:22–23)

We are his body. What a vivid image of who and what we are. The body has many parts and the parts have many functions. Similarly, the church in the world has the promise of the presence of Christ and we are his body. The New Testament goes to some lengths to define and explain who we are as the church.

If we take seriously this frequently used biblical metaphor of the church as body, we must acknowledge that every part of the body is necessary for it to function as a whole. The church, of course, is centered on the person of Jesus Christ who is the "head" of the body. But our faith journey is lived out in the community of believers called the church. I agree with Maxie Dunnam, president of Asbury Theological Semenary, who believes that "there is no Christianity apart from the church."[4] A Christian is someone who has a personal relationship with Jesus Christ and the relationship is lived out in a community called the church.

When we interview a person for a position on our staff, one of their first questions is "What is the job description?" "If I accept this position what is expected of me?" Similarly, if we are to live out our Christian faith with others in community, what is expected of us? Sociologist Robert Wuthnow, in a helpful book entitled *Christianity in the 21st Century*, has described what we should be doing as we live out our faith together in the church. He says we should be

Celebrating Christ in our worship

Honoring Christ in our work

Revealing Christ in our walk, witness, and fellowship

Instructing persons for discipleship and ministry

Transforming the world by spreading the word of Jesus Christ[5]

Our life, our work, our worship, and our teaching should be done to equip all members of the church for the proclamation of the gospel. The place where each of us experiences, "the body of Christ" is the local, particular church of which we are members. We all know that the "local" expression of the church is a mixed bag and that there are some "imperfect" people who are members. The church militant often feels like the church hesitant. When the Bible speaks of "God's peculiar people," we immediately think of some of the folks in the church where we are striving to live out our faith.

We are not perfect but one of the most worn-out excuses for nonparticipation in the church is that "there are so many hypocrites in the church." This may be true, but can you think of a better place for a hypocrite to be? At least in church there is the chance that the spirit of God might move someone from hypocrisy to sincerity. The church is not a museum for the display of saints but a school for the nurture of sinners.

In all of our humanity, and Christ knew it when he described who we are, he still called us his body. We are

His ears to hear the cries of those who need us and who need Christ

His voice to tell the story of his love and to speak for those who have no voice, who will never be heard unless we speak on their behalf

His hands to lift the fallen and his feet to go where there is need

His heart to respond to needs and inner conflicts

His head to create plans to reach those who do not know his name

We are the body of Christ. When we review that description of who we are in the mind of Christ, we are both humbled by the privilege and overwhelmed by the reponsibility. In our church we can be, and should be, a voice, and we sometimes are the only voice where we live and work. If we are silent, we can make no difference. Just think that Christ's work might not be done if we are not at work in the Savior's name. Realize that if our ears are deaf to the cries of need, those who cry out may not receive help. His plans will not be fulfilled if our heart and mind is not attuned to the needs around us. Every one of us is somebody in the church, the body of Christ, and the work of the church is to be done by everybody, not somebody else.

We occasionally plan what we call a "Super Saturday of Service" at Peachtree Presbyterian. Super Saturday requires many volunteers and a great deal of coordination, but it is a day of joy for all who participate. On this particular Saturday, we mobilized more than nine hundred people who visit thirty places of need. We repair some houses that needed repairs, we put a roof on one house, we built a ramp for easy access for a person who was confined to a wheelchair. We also visited the Atlanta Food Bank to package food that will be made available at low cost to those who need it and we painted walls at an elementary school in the inner city where we have been at work for several years. At more than thirty locations throughout the city, the body of Christ that is Peachtree Presbyterian Church, was at work for God and for good.

If we can begin to think of ourselves in church as "The Body of Christ," it will enhance our sense of responsibility for the work we are called upon to perform. The body of Christ is mobilized in a world that is not always responsive to who and what we are. Theologian Karl Rahner said that the chief function of the church is to be a "community," and to provide community, a place where people feel cared for and are able to care for others. He believed that the church is "the visible sign of salvation that God has established in this seemingly godless world."

The Church's Challenges

As members of the church, when we engage our community in the proclamtion of the gospel, we face a number of challenges, one of which is the pace of change. The old adage that there is nothing as certain as "death and taxes" may be substantially true but it is also true that there is nothing more predictable or certain than change itself.

As a result of technological change, we live in a global village. In this context, the church must be a "community of memory" so that as Robert Wuthnow said, "individuals will know who they are and for what purpose they are living."[6] Stanley Hauerwas of Duke Divinity School said that the church is a "community of moral discourse, a community that sustains the ongoing implications of its commitments across generations as it faces new challenges."[7]

At Peachtree Presbyterian, we have 3,000 members in their twenties, many of whom are experiencing church for the first time with us. They have caused us to change the way we do things. They provide the challenge of honest questions and the energy to engage in programs and projects that require their energy. New members can do this in every church.

The church must not only engage this kind of change but redeem it as well. The basic hungers of the human heart are still the same. Many people hunger for "certainties" that give both security and hope. The changes in some ways accentuate the spiritual quest that is going on all around us. What a great time to proclaim and live out the gospel of Jesus Christ.

A church can also benefit from new technologies to proclaim the gospel and fulfill its mission. For example, we now use the Internet to communicate with our college students and keep them informed as to what is going on in the church. Our youth ministers correspond with them by way of "e-mail" all the time. These high-tech tools can be used to give "high touch" to the church's care of its members who are away from home. The changes are upon us and we must move beyond coping to turning them to the church's advantage. Some churches proclaim the gospel through a Web Page that provides information about who they are, what they are doing, and the text of recent sermons.

While some might say the church should reflect tradition and do things the old way, we must not fear change. G. K. Chesterton observed about Christianity that "The more I considered Christianity, the more I have found that while it had established rule and order, the chief aim of that order was to give room for good things to run wild.[8]

Isn't that wonderful? The church can create a climate "for good things to run wild." In response to the changes that are already here and coming, in the future, we can increasingly become "change agents" for Christ.

The increasing secular indifference to the church is both a challenge and an opportunity. We are finding it difficult to proclaim the gospel in a time when the mainline church is losing its place. It is often ignored, and considered irrelevant to the "real world." The secular world is raising questions that we must face and answer but the real danger is that we will opt for the "world's agenda." It is obvious that we cannot ignore the world but we must not conform to its wishes and priorities.

There was a time when the church was relied on as a moral force but that was then and this is now. We have given an ambivalent message, have wavered on moral issues, and sought some comfortable accommondation on many issues when we should have been pointing the way.

The times of challenge that we face will be good for us. The most effective way for us to reach people who have no real sense of their need for religion is to demonstrate to them, by the quality of our lives, that we have been with Jesus and he has made us whole. There are changes that challenge the church. There is a growing religious diversity in this country, there is the crowding in the inner cities, there is the mindless madness that stalks our streets, and there is the breakdown of the family unit. People often ask me "Are you discouraged?" My answer is "No, I am challenged." I frankly think that it is going to be good for the church to face the challenge of proclaiming the gospel in an unchurched society. We are challenged to have a faith that is both real and transforming in our lives before we can proclaim our faith to others. There are encouraging signs. George Barna does research on American religious issues and annually publishes *The Index of Leading Spiritual Indicators*. His data encourages me and it resonates consistently with what I am experiencing. Barna notes that . . .

> Three out of four Americans say having a close relationship with God is very desirable
>
> Thirty percent of Americans strongly believe they have a personal responsibility to tell others about their faith
>
> half of all American adults believe it is very desirable to belong to a congregation

in any given week, 25 percent of Americans are exposed to the Christian media by means of television, radio, books, or magazines.[9]

This wave of seekers who is looking for spiritual sustenance is the church's great opportunity as it faces a new century. I believe that the church will rise to the challenge of this opportunity. The question is how?

I believe the "how" is found in the promises that undergird our work. We are the "body of Christ" (I Corinthians 12:27) and Christ has promised that "where two or thre are gathered together in my name I am gathered there among them" (Matthew 18:20).

A young woman, a medical resident, lost her child. She later became the head of Pediatric Cardiology in a large university hospital. When asked what lead her into pediatric cardiology, she responded by saying the day her baby died, the pediatric cardiologist who was her supervisor and teacher reached out to her. She said "He came over to me the day my baby died and put his arms around me, and I remember thinking he's the only person who did that."[10]

We proclaim the gospel with power when we respond to the needs of people and when we busy ourselves putting our arms around people who suffer. It is the capacity of the church and its people to be a caring presence in the world that undergirds our proclamation. We are, after all, *ekklesia*, the "called out ones," called out to proclaim and to care. "We love because He first loved us" (I John 4:19). It is our loving response that opens the doors to the hearts of people. We live under the powerful promises of our Savior that we shall be victorious. Christians, and the Christian church do not give up. The call is for an ever-deepening commitment to Christ, and the mandate is clear: "preach, teach and make disciples" (Matthew 28:19). We have never had a greater opportunity to do just that than we have today.

Charles Colson, convicted of Watergate crimes, organized The Prison Fellowship when his prison time was over. Many doubted his conversion to Christianity but the record is clear today of the breadth and depth of his ministry. One day, Colson and others were visiting an Indiana prison where incorrigibles were confined. He was making a hasty trip and he had a pressing appointment that he did not want to miss.

The group was on the way out of the prison and came to the last security point when Colson noticed that one of the volunteers in his prison ministry, a judge, was missing. He looked around and saw the judge in conversation with one of the prisoners. Colson called out, "We've got to get going! I've got a tight schedule!" The judge said he would be ready in a minute or two. A minute or two stretched into five minutes, and Colson, more edgy, insisted they leave. The judge replied: "I understand but I need time to have prayer with this man, for I am the judge who sentenced him to die in the electric chair. James here is now a Christian, a brother in Christ, and we want to have a minute to pray with each other!"[11]

Judge and death row inmate, together, united in Christ, prayed with and for each other. A scene like that could not and would not take place apart from the Church of Jesus Christ. The church is first, last, and always a transforming fellowship.

For Reflection and Discussion

1. Do you believe or sense in your community that we live more and more in an unchurched society?

2. As you experience the church where you are a member, does it feel like "the body of Christ?" If it does, what is the most obvious evidence of Christ you see in its fellowship and mission? If not, what is missing?

3. Is your church a "visible sign of salvation" in your community? How?

4. What changes do you see in your community that will challenge your church to change its program to meet new needs? Are you ready and willing to engage those changes?

5. List five reasons why someone would want to come to the church where you are a member.

6. Are you encouraged or discouraged about your church? If encouraged, are you telling others about the joy you are experiencing? If discouraged, are you actively engaged with the pastor and key leaders in turning things around?

7. How is your church proclaiming the gospel in its Christian Service in your community?

8. How are you experiencing the changes in society in your church?

9. What are you doing to reach out to an unchurched world?

10. Does the proclamation of the gospel in your church speak to the unchurched?

PART II
The Basics

5

The Bible—The Source of Our Proclamation

"The whole Bible was given to us by inspiration of God and is useful to teach us what is true and to make us realize what is wrong in our lives; it straightens us out and helps us do what is right." (2 Timothy 3:16, *The Living Bible*)

I first became aware of the Bible because my father read from it to us every evening before bedtime. It was a regular part of our family life. My father's Bible was well marked and underlined and contained his handwritten comments in the margins. He also put a mark by the chapter headings indicating the number of times he had read that particular chapter. It was obvious to me that it was an important book. My familiarity with the Bible grew as my mother read the stories of the Bible to me and as I memorized its verses in Sunday School. It was natural for me in my own family to read the Bible myself and to read its stories to our two daughters and now to our three grandchildren.

On a July evening in 1961, I was ordained and affirmed this vow: "Do you believe the Holy Scriptures, in the original languages of the Old and New Testaments, are the only infallible rule of faith and practice?" I said yes then, and I say yes today!

The Bible is God's word for the church. I think about its centrality each Sunday as the services of worship begin at Peachtree Presbyterian. The hour is struck for the service to begin, and as the chimes are sounded, an elder comes down the center aisle to place the Bible, the Scriptures of the Old and New Testament on the communion table. It is the word of God. Inscribed on the central pulpit in our sanctuary is this verse from Peter:

"The Word Of The Lord Endures Forever!"
(I Peter 1:25)

Why emphasize the Bible? Because the Bible contains the story we are to proclaim. The Bible is the story of God's relationship to his people and the story of God's persistence through wars, famine, pestilence, loyalty, and disloyalty. God persisted in his capacity to love us even though his law was violated. His words were ignored, his desires were abandoned, and his plans were scuttled by our duplicity and our indifference. Yet God persisted because his love never lets us go and it never lets us off. God made full and final disclosure of his great heart of love in sending his only Son, Jesus Christ, our Savior. We find the story of all of this in the Bible. The Bible contains the content of our proclamation.

Unfortunately, the Bible is honored by many but seldom read. There is an unbelievable ignorance of the Bible today and those of us who preach cannot assume anything when we use it as the foundation of a sermon. There will be people in the congregation on any given Sunday who will not have any idea who Jacob and Esau are or what their rivalry is all about. What was the struggle between their parents all about? Why did their mother favor Jacob over the other twin Esau? The *Atlanta Journal Constitution* of July 26, 1997, ran an article by Gayle White that contained the results of a poll conducted by the newspaper on the nation's reading habits of the Bible. The poll indicated that 49.7 percent of Presbyterians read the Bible regularly as compared to 49 percent of United Methodists, 35.9 percent of Lutherans, and 32.4 percent of Roman Catholics.[1]

The poll also revealed that people in the South read the Bible more often that non-Southerners. For example, 16 percent of Southerners read the Bible daily, whereas 9 percent of non-Southerners do. Southern women read the Bible daily at a higher percentage than men (22 percent for women, 11 percent for men). Twenty-eight percent of African-American women read the Bible daily as compared to only fourteen percent of the men. And another twenty percent of Southerners read the Bible two to six times every week; whereas only ten percent of non-Southerners. Finally, Southerners sixty-five and older are three times more likely to read the Bible daily than those who are twenty-nine and under.[2]

It has long been obvious that the Bible is important in, and religiously central to, the culture of the South. Americans value the Bible as a part of their heritage even though, like the rest of the country, they often profess more faith than they practice. It is a constant temptation to do so, just as if you are a clergy person, it is a constant temptation to preach more faith than you possess.

We value the Bible but candor requires that I acknowledge, for most people, the Bible remains, to quote scholar Peter Gomes, "an elusive, unknown, slightly daunting book." I have many parishioners say to me, "I wish I knew more about the Bible." We respond to that need by offering courses in the basics of the Bible. This unfamiliarity exists despite the multitude of versions and translations available to people of all ages.[3] John Calvin said that "the Bible is the lens through which Christians view all reality." It is, therefore, not an inconsequential thing that there is such widespread ignorance of the Bible.

Why has biblical knowledge decreased rather than increased? Is it because the emphasis on scripture is not as strong as it used to be in the American Church? I believe that is true, but only you can speak for your own church in your particular place. A recent poll by the Barna Research Group revealed that of a sample of more that 1,000 persons, 10 percent said that Joan of Arc was Noah's wife and 38 percent were convinced that both the Old and New Testaments were written a few years after the death of Jesus of Nazareth.[4]

Peter Gomes, in his recent and helpful book entitled *The Good Book*, is on target when he compares many contemporary Christians with the emperor

Charlemagne. Charlemagne is reported to have slept with a copy of Saint Augustine's *The City of God* under his pillow. He did so in the hope that his passive closeness to this great and difficult theological work might be of some benefit to him.[5]

I am convinced that people value the Bible. In the church which I serve, we regularly have to replenish the supply of pew Bibles. Where do they go? People just carry a copy home with them. If you feel shocked, I do also, but upon reflection, if someone is going to walk off with something to read, the Bible is not a bad choice. We value the Bible but many never read it. It is a kind of ready file folder for clippings we want to save or pictures that we value. There is an ambivalence about the Bible and we cannot allow the situation to continue, for as evangelist Dr. Billy Graham recently said:

> "One of the greatest tragedies today is that, although the Bible is an available, open book, it is a closed book to millions—either because they leave it unread or because they read it without applying its teachings to themselves. No greater tragedy can befall humankind or a nation than that of paying lip service to a Bible left unread or a way of life not followed."[6]

The Importance of Teaching the Bible

If we are to take seriously the "proclamation of the gospel" as the first of the Great Ends of the Church, then we must take seriously the Bible as the content of our faith. It is the Bible that gives us a story to tell. We must introduce those we are trying to reach to an awareness of the Bible and encourage them, through our churches, to read it, study it, and listen for the voice of God to speak to them through the Bible. It is, after all, a lamp for our feet and a light for our path.

It is interesting that our theme verse for this chapter finds Paul, the Apostle, writing to his well-loved protégé Timothy about the Bible. Timothy was a third-generation Christian. The scriptures that Paul was talking about were Old Testament scriptures. Timothy had been taught them by his grandmother and his mother. Paul says to Timothy that he "should keep on believing the things he had been taught" (II Timothy 3:14).

Please note that Timothy had been taught as a child (II Timothy 3:15). It is interesting to me that we can work ourselves into frantic concern over the secular education of our children and give little thought to their Christian education. Recently, a concerned mother came to me and said that her two boys would miss Sunday School for some months because soccer practice on Sunday morning conflicted with Sunday School. What was she to do? I reminded her that we have three sessions of Sunday School and her boys could take their pick. Surely soccer practice did not last all Sunday morning? I also suggested that she just might forego soccer, observing that Sunday School participation might be more important than soccer. Where are today's Timothys?

The question is one of priorities in every family with small children. To teach the Bible or not to teach it. It is a priority in every person's life, to make the commitment to Christ or not to commit. We proclaim the gospel for a verdict, a choice, and a commitment to Christ, and a part of that proclamation is the content of the faith, the Bible. We would not know about Jesus Christ were it not for the Bible.

In their initial contact with the Bible, those to whom we proclaim the gospel will have two basic questions.

First they will ask "Who wrote the Bible?" The Bible was written by holy persons inspired by God to write down the stories. God did not dictate the stories to a scribe. Holy persons felt "led by the Spirit" to write down their experiences of God. Each writer in the books of the Bible brought his or her unique style and personality. They were used by God to tell the story. The books of the Bible, generally speaking, grew out of a unique set of circumstances.[7]

We use the work "inspiration" to mean that the spirit of God influenced the writers. The inspiration of God means that we can depend on the Bible as words of truth. The spirit of God led the biblical writers to set down matters of faith and inspiration in a dependable fashion because God was "breathing into" their work his will and his truth.[8] So when we place this Holy Bible on the communion table in our sanctuary, and when we read from it and hold it up, it means that we hold on to and rely on this book.

The Bible is not just another book. It is God's book. It is, in fact, a collection of books—sixty-six of them—collected from the writings of the ancient Hebrews and the early Christians over a period of centuries.[9] It is the product of a divine human process that produced it as "the gift of God for the people of God."

The second question people ask is "Why was the Bible written?" I believe it was written to lead us to our salvation. It was written to tell us of God's love and how his love persisted through the centuries. We are, in the church, the "people of the book," the Bible. As we read it and study it, we should be reminded of the words of that well-loved hymn we sing:

" . . . breathe on me, breath of God,
Fill me with life anew,
that I may love what thou dost love,
and do what thou wouldst do!"

Theologian Georgia Harkness has succinctly stated that

"The scriptures are the record of God's progressive revelation of Himself through inspired men and the story of the righteous purpose in history to bring (humankind) to final perfection in Christ. The Bible contains all that God requires for salvation and is the sufficient rule of faith and conduct. It has withstood all efforts to destroy it; it has survived the scientific study of its pages, and by its enduring truth it has confounded its critics and stands today more historically credible and more spiritually indispensable than ever before. It is God's eternal word to every generation."[10]

What the Bible Provides

The Bible is God's word and a guide for faithful living. It essentially provides four things:

1. Doctrine—What God wants us to know
    Paul writes to Timothy and says, "the whole Bible was given to us by inspiration from God and is useful to teach us what is true." (II Timothy 3:16—*The Living Bible*).

    The Bible is about God, God's love, and how his love was fully revealed to us through Jesus Christ. We read the Bible and sometimes do not like what it wants us to do. In response, we have a tendency to want to pick and choose the passages that support our bias or our lifestyle. In our quest for individualism, we tend to conveniently forget that "God's ways are not our ways and his thoughts are not our thoughts." Our culture is not the standard by which our Bible is measured. Our Bible is, in fact, the standard by which we should measure our faith and conduct. The Ten Commandments, for example, are not random suggestions. They are *commandments*, and to ignore them is not so much to break them as to be broken by them if we neglect their truth.

    We often go to the Bible with the wrong questions or premises. The Bible reflects its historical time and context but articulates its truth in that context in timeless, ageless principles of truth. One of the characters in *Alice In Wonderland* is a lock. It is a very restless, frustrated lock. It could not be still. It was engaged in a rather frantic and endless search. Alice observed what was going on and raised the obvious question: "What is the matter?" The lock replied "I am seeking for something to unlock me!"[11] We can find in the Bible many keys that will open doors in our lives, unlocking our potential to love, to share, to aspire, and to hope.

I have found in my journey, as have many others that I have known, comfort and strength in the Bible. I recall one day recently when visiting one of our nursing homes in Atlanta that as I gave communion to one of our members who lives there, she quoted along with me the words of institution for The Lord's Supper. She recalled clearly the words of the 23rd Psalm as I quoted it after we had shared the Sacred Supper. As I prepared to leave after the visit, she said "Thanks for coming. I feel a great peace!"

Was it the sacrament or the words of the Bible? It was both and both are essential for the church in its proclamation of the gospel. The Bible comforts us by reminding us that God wants to stand with us and walk with us through any challenge or sorrow. We will not understand everything that we read in the Bible, but the Bible can and does strengthen our resolve in the face of challenge and adversity. Karl Barth, noted Twentieth-century theologian, felt that the church in Germany during the rise of Hitler did not measure up to the test or accept its responsibility. When it was time to say "No," the church faltered. In fact it had said "Yes" too often. Barth felt the church lacked the resources of faith to be steadfast in its stand for truth. In response to this crisis in his nation, Barth participated in the writing of the *Barmen Declaration* which begins with these words:

"Jesus Christ, as he is attested for us in Holy Scripture, is the one Word of God which we have to hear and which we have to trust in life and in death. We reject as false doctrine (that the church) . . . would have to acknowledge as a source of its proclamation apart from and besides this one Word of God . . . "[12]

The word of God can and will stiffen our "theological spines" when we are threatened and tempted by the cultural captivity of the church in our time or any time. The Bible provides a framework for us, giving us doctrine, what God wants us to know.

2. Reproof—What God wants us to stop doing

The Bible also gives us the framework for proper living. Paul writes to his young friend Timothy, "The whole Bible . . . is useful to teach us what is true and to make us realize what is wrong in our lives. . . ." (II Timothy 3:16—*The Living Bible*).

We find instructions in the Bible as to how we are to relate to God. "You shall have no other gods before me." We are told how we are to relate to each other. We are to love and honor parents, relate faithfully to our spouses, to value the life of others, and not to covet what others have that we do not have. We are not to speak falsehoods about another, and we are to set aside a day for the worship and praise of God. All that is needed for proper living is there in the Bible for our nurture and nourishment.

3. Correction—What God wants us to change

Paul reminds Timothy that the scriptures "make us realize what is wrong in our lives" (II Timothy 3:16—*The Living Bible*). The things that are wrong need to be made right. God wants us to change, to get right. His word is a lamp so that we will "set our feet in the right directions." It is a light so that we will not make our way into dark places. When we proclaim the gospel, we are challenged to change. We have to change if things are to be made new.

I have three grandchildren one granddaughter and two grandsons. Our youngest grandchild, James, has difficulty at age three understanding why everything does not go his way. He often gets frustrated with his older brother and sister and they sometimes encourage his frustration. More often than not, however, James just wants things to go his way. I picked him up recently when he was crying, great tears running down his cheeks and asked "What is the matter, why are you crying?" He said through his tears as he put his head on my shoulder, "I want to do it my way."

Isn't that the story of each of our lives? We would like to do things "our way" and that often results in tears. If we are to walk with Christ, we must change to get some things right. We read the words of Christ so easily but they represent tremendous change. For example, " . . . turn the other cheek," "walk the second mile," "do to those who persecute you," and "love your enemies."

So easy to say, to read, so difficult to accomplish! Jesus' teachings represent a radical departure from the ways of the world: "tit for tat," "eye for an eye," "tooth for a tooth." In the days just before Desert Storm, a pastor in the morning prayer prayed for the people of "Iraq, and for all people who live in conditions of the threat of war." Afterward, he was confronted by an angry person who found the prayer offensive and said to him "Don't you realize that we must stand behind our troops in Saudi Arabia? How dare you lift up, in such a positive way, the people who are our sworn enemies."[13]

One wonders if the person accosting the pastor knew the Bible or had hearts of the instruction to "pray for our enemies." Christ calls us to radical change in our lives and sends us forth, in his name, to make radical changes in our world. We are cynical at times about how we respond to Christ's call for change. We tend to sluff it off by saying "that was then, this is now." Or we say, "Yea the lion might lie down with the lamb, but the lamb is going to spend a very restless night."

We are called upon to read our Bible and share our faith in a time when society around us advances ideas and propositions that are opposed to what we are trying to live and proclaim. The unspoken proposition today is that only scientific or factual knowledge is real knowledge. The hidden message is that Biblical knowledge may not be real or even reliable. Therefore, beliefs that are not based on scientific facts are opinions at best, and are not to be trusted.

The fact that we rely more and more on science and technology does not mean that we are less spiritual. In fact, the case can be made that the more we are dependent on or dominated by, our technology, the more acute our spiritual needs become. The basic hungers of the human spirit cannot be met by mere technology. We must resist the premise many hold that our beliefs have the status of mere opinion because they are not validated by science. It is so easy to scorn our "religious beliefs" as not having real standing in an age of technology. Nothing could be further from the truth. We are in need of something more in our lives to give meaning and purpose.

It is my experience that most people yearn for some *inner* certainties in the midst of a world that seems uncertain. The Bible asserts that "in the world we will have tribulation," trouble, hardship, and uncertainty. The answer of the Bible is not to abandon the world or request to be taken out of this world but rather to ask God to give us the strength to boldly speak the truth of God in this world and to live our lives as models of what God would have us be. How can we do that? We can be strengthened and encouraged by the one who said: "Be of good cheer for I have overcome the world." (John 16:33).

Michael Green, an Anglican clergyperson, said in his study of proclamation and evangelism in the early church, "They (the early Christians) made the grace of God credible by a society of love and mutual care which astonished the pagans and was recognized as something entirely new. It lent persuasiveness to their claim that the new age had dawned in Christ."[14]

This is also our task in our time and the Bible is our guide. Another side of science also bothersome to "religious belief" in our time is a growing sense that our use of technology gives us complete control over our destiny, not to mention our lives. Yet, not many people who come to see me in my study say "I have everything I need! I am the master of my fate, the captain of my soul." To the contrary, they say "something is missing; there's got to be more than what I have."

E. B. White described hearing the deep departing blast of the horn of the ocean liner *Queen Mary*, at midnight: "the sound carried the whole history of departure, longing, and loss."[15] "Departure, longing, and loss." What can voice mail do for them? It conveys a voice on a machine. God never puts you or me on hold! He is the one "who never slumbers nor sleeps." The God of the Bible is always listening with loving ears, seeing with gentle eyes, and reaching to take our hands in his.

Anne Dillard, in her book *Holy The Firm*, draws a dramatic picture of the dilemma of picking the church that you want to join and attend. She comes to the conclusion that nothing is more convincing of God's unending mercy than the continued existence of the church.[16]

She draws a distinction between what she calls the "higher Christian churches" and the "low Christian churches." In the higher churches she says the people come to God with an "unwarranted air of professionalism, with authority, and pomp." In "higher" worship, they tiptoe along like people walking atop a "strand of scaffolding" who have long ago forgotten how dangerous that can be. If God were to interrupt such a high service, the people would be shocked. The "low church" is different, for there you expect God to "blast such a service to bits" any minute. And, as Dillard concludes, " . . . this is the beginning of wisdom!"[17]

The Bible, from beginning to end, on page after page, is urging fundamental change in our lives because of Jesus Christ. God's loving heart is reaching out to us and has made ample provision for us and our needs.

4. Instructions in Righteousness

We are to be "equipped" for service, "furnished" with everything that is needed. It is encouraging to believe that we are going to be provided everything we need as we make our faith journey. It is an assurance that we can give to those to whom we tell the story for it is easy to get discouraged as we wait.

Sometimes, however, waiting is the answer. There is a Chinese proverb that says of the Bible "whoever made this book made me." The Bible will mold and make us after God's will for our lives, which is not always consistent with our wishes for our lives. In South Africa some years ago, the government of Pretoria issued a decree banning the lighting of candles and the singing of Christmas carols in Soweto. The press raised questions about this and the government replied "You know how emotional black women are. Christmas carols have an emotional impact upon them." (*St. Louis Dispatch*, December 27, 1985.). Just think of the restricted, oppressed people of Soweto lighting candles and singing on Christmas eve the song that Mary, the mother of Jesus, sang when she knew that she was to carry a special, holy child: "He has shown strength with his arms; he has scattered the proud in the thoughts of their hearts. He has brought down the powerful from their thrones, and lifted up the lowly" (Luke 1:15–52)[18]

The Bible promises us that we will be equipped to do the work that God has called us to do. We will be empowered as we trust him to be all that he would have us be. Our proclamation is to encourage all of us to walk with Christ in our daily lives and to make the Bible our handbook for living. On October 5, 1995, Pope John Paul II addressed the United Nations and gave us all some encouraging words:

"We must not be afraid of the future. We must not be afraid of (mankind). It is no accident that we are here. Each and every human person has been created in the "image and likeness of the One who is the original of all that is. We have within us the capacities for wisdom and virtue. With these gifts, and with the help of

God's grace, we can build in the next century
and the next millennium a civilization worthy of
the human person, a true culture of freedom.
We can and must do so! And in doing so, we
shall see that the tears of this century have
prepared the ground for a new springtime of
the human spirit."

It is time for us and for the church to stand up to
proclaim the Bible's power and ask the people who hear
our proclamation to let this word of God have a chance
in our hearts and in our lives.

For Reflection and Discussion

1. Do your children have a working knowledge of the Bible?
2. Have they recently read through the Bible?
3. When was the last time you read:
   The four Gospels?
   The Psalms?
   Proverbs?
4. Do you read your Bible daily?
5. Is you church providing a parish of Bible study for your
   people? All race groups?

6

Your Convictions About Jesus Christ are Essential

"God raised Him up to the heights of heaven and gave Him a name which is above every name." (Philippians 2:9—*The Living Bible*)

In Jesus Christ, we have the full and final disclosure of all that God is. If you want a clear picture of God's heart, motives, and love, take a look at Jesus Christ. Jesus Christ is my Lord and Savior; he is Lord and head of the church.

Almost from the time Jesus was born, a persistent question has dominated people's interest: "Who is this Jesus?" For example:

when Jesus helped a paralyzed man, saying to him, "your sins are forgiven you," the Pharisees who were present raised an immediate question—"Who is this that speaks such blasphemies?" (Luke 5:20–21)

when Jesus stilled the storm on the Sea of Galilee, his astonished and relieved disciples raised the question: "Who is this man, that even wind and waves obey?" (Mark 4:41)

when Herod began to hear the details of his ministry, having recently beheaded John the Baptist, he said, "Who is this about whom I hear such things?" (Luke 9:9)

when Jesus entered Jerusalem on that first Palm Sunday to great acclaim and celebrations, the whole city stirred around one central question: "Who is this?" (Matthew 21:10)

This question, "Who is this Jesus?" continues today, as newspaper and magazine stories attest. It is raised because Christianity rests foundationally on that question. As British theologian John R. Stott, has pointed out "Christianity is the only religion in the world which rests on the Person of its founder."[1] And H. P. Liddon, Chancellor of St. Paul's Cathedral in London, said of Jesus "his most startling revelation was Himself."[2]

Jesus' Gifts to Us

Our theme verse from Philippians 2:9 is one of the most vivid descriptions of Christ and his work in the Bible. This section of the letter to the Philippians is called "The Christ Hymn" and many scholars believed that it was actually sung as part of the worship of the early church. It describes fully what Christ has provided for us and for our salvation. It is this essential message that we proclaim when we live and preach the gospel. In Jesus' Incarnation, Crucifixion, and Resurrection, we have been provided all that we need for our salvation.

The Incredible Incarnation

John's gospel opens dramatically: "The word became flesh and dwelt among us" (John 1:14). There it is in a sentence. He came, he experienced, he knew what it was like to be fully human. When he mashed his finger in his father's woodworking shop, it hurt and it bled. At the end of a demanding day, he was tired. He knew the affirmation of friends who brought him joy. He experienced the rebuff of his hometown and knew rejection. He knew what temptations were all about and the sustaining presence of God in dealing with them. The Bible simply says of him "he knows our frame and remembers that we are dust." How did he know that? He knew it because he was human.

The German theologian and martyr Dietrich Bonhoeffer said that in Jesus Christ "the message and the messenger became one." If I were God and planning to send my son to earth, I would have done it differently. I would not have sent him to a backwater town like Nazareth. The common saying in the region was that nothing good could come out of Nazareth. If you really wanted to make a dramatic arrival statement, Nazareth was not the place. Of course, Jesus was born in Bethlehem which had some history, but who would want to mix up the birth of the Son of God with a government census and more taxes for Rome?

My first choice for the place of Jesus' birth would have been Rome. It was the center of the known world and the seat of earthly power. Rome and its people were the center of world power and culture. It was a worthy place for the Son of God to be born. He would confront Caesar on his own turf. My second choice would have been Athens, Greece, the seat of culture, philosophy, architecture, and oratory. My third choice would have been Jerusalem, the seat of religion, the Holy City. Jews all over the world made annual pilgrimages to Jerusalem. Word of the Son of God's coming would have passed quickly to the far regions of the earth.

Rome; Athens; Jerusalem. But it was not any of these. Instead, he came quietly, surprisingly, as P. T. Forsyth said "Our real and destined eternity goes round by Nazareth to reach you and me."[3]

The appeal of Christ to us is not one of demand but of love. He is not distant but near. He has promised to stand with us whatever the time or condition: "I am with you always" (Luke 18:16). He is a king like no other who came before him or since. This is why we reckon time as being before his birth and after he came. He was godly but gently. He was passionate but patient. He was chastised because he cared. He had a demanding ministry but was never too busy not to "turn aside" to respond to the hurts of those who called to him. Little children loved him and he loved them and had a standing order with his disciples: "let the children come to me and do not hinder them" (Matthew 19:14). One of his sternest warnings concerned how we treat children. He said "if anyone caused any of these little ones to stumble, it would be better that they have a great rock tied around their necks and they be cast into the sea" (Mark 9:42). He looked for the genuine expression of religion, not public show. His delight was in the substance of faith, not in the form. He was not a practiced orator but he drew crowds because he "spoke with authority and not like the Scribes and Pharisees" (Matthew 7:29). The result was "the common people heard him gladly" (Mark 12:37).

The Centrality of Calvary

We cannot consider Christ without the reality of the cross. They put him to death on a cross outside the city walls. They placed him between two thieves. It was there that he died with people jeering, spitting, drinking, attracted to the spectacle of an execution. There were three of them there, but the principle focus was the one labeled "the king of the Jews" (Luke 23:38).

One of the most fascinating figures in the drama of the final week of our Lord's life was the Roman centurion who commanded the detail of legionnaires that escorted Jesus to Calvary, the place of death. He was an experienced soldier. He must have seen Jesus' dramatic arrival in the city and must have thought there could be trouble before the week was over. This centurion must also have seen Jesus' confrontations with the religious leaders and the tense debate that characterized the exchanges. And when Jesus upset the tables of the moneychangers in the city, the centurion knew that trouble *had* arrived. Jesus had hit them in the pocketbook where it hurt. The centurion would have noted the growing size and excitement of the crowd that followed Jesus everywhere, sensed the growing tension in the city, and seen the late-night arrivals and departures from the places of power in government and religion.

The centurion was a participant in Jesus' arrest and stood guard while the accusers committed perjury, not only not telling the truth, but also fabricating charges against him. The centurion would have noticed the quiet courage of this man Jesus who did not open his mouth in his own defense. Although a hardened soldier of many campaigns, the centurion had never seen anything like what unfolded at the place of death. The man Jesus prayed for those who planned and carried out his trial and sentencing and even consoled one of the thieves. He also noted that Jesus was concerned about his mother who had to witness the cruel death of her son.

The centurion watched as Jesus died and felt ashamed that his own men were gambling for his meager possessions. This hardened soldier looked once into the penetrating eyes of Jesus of Nazareth and what he saw was not a man losing his life, but one who was giving his life. When he breathed his last, the centurion heard him say "It is finished."

As the centurion walked away, he had come to a fundamental decision about the man on the central cross. His observation immortalized him: "Surely, this man was the Son of God." (Mark 15:39).

There is no historical record to affirm what I am about to say, but I believe that this centurion became a believer. How could he resist?

Do we take Jesus and his death for granted? I know that "by his stripes we are healed." I know that he was "bruised for our iniquities." I know that the Lord "has laid on him the iniquity of us all." And yet, I wonder if we have not come to the place where we take it all for granted. It has been a part of our culture, our heritage for so long, that we hardly stop to notice. What does it mean that crosses are in great demand today as jewelry? I cannot discern whether that is a plus or a negative. A cross is not an ornament to be hung around our necks.

Reverend Roberta Corson of Campbell, California, tells about a family with a two-year-old child who attended church one Sunday. During the service, the children were invited to come forward to hear a story. When the story was over, all of the children rushed back to be with their parents. All but one; this little girl. She stood alone in the center of the chancel gazing at the stained glass window. She was not fidgety or chatty; she simply stood there in silence looking at the window, trying to take it all in.

She was utterly silent and soon the entire church was silent. The child stood there quietly, focused on the window. What did she see? Did she see something that the others had never seen before? Was it the light radiating through the window? Was it the high vaulted ceiling that framed the window? Was it the whole sense of the presence and mystery of God that everyone was talking about? After a long time, she turned and quietly retuned to sit by her parents. All who attended church that day knew that they have been in the presence of God in a special way. A holy moment had descended upon their worship; something had happened that had not been printed in the bulletin.[4]

I feel just like the pastor must have felt that day. Our children are more open to the Holy Spirit than most of us. She had not yet been conditioned to take it all for granted, to let the spirit brush over us, and not enter into us. We must never forget that the bleeding on Calvary on that dreaded day was the heart of God bleeding for you and for me.

The Resurrection

I am moved by the way Jesus Christ came and by his incredible incarnation. I am aware in my own spirit of the centrality of Calvary but I am sustained and given hope by his amazing resurrection. "He is not here . . . He is risen" (Matthew 28:6). It is the most dramatic announcement ever made. If the resurrection is not true, then we have no gospel to proclaim, no salvation to offer to anyone. This strong current of hope sweeps through us and in us with the approach of Easter each year. The resurrection gives birth to our hopes.

We are the "resurrection people." We worship on Sunday in the Christian church because every time we worship, it is a celebration of the resurrection. When the community of faith gathers to say goodbye to one who has completed their earthly journey, the service begins with this statement of victory:

> "This service is in witness to the resurrection of Jesus Christ and in grateful celebration for the life of _____ , because Christ lives we shall live also."

Thoughts of what now and what next always come to us when death intrudes into our lives. Where can we go but to Christ and the assuring promise of his resurrection? As we tell the story of all that Christ has provided for us, the story demands a decision, a commitment. One cannot stay neutral forever. He came, He conquered, and we are called upon to respond.

God's reign is rooted in the reality of the resurrection. It is the resurrection that sends us out with joy to proclaim the gospel's challenge and hope. In *The Summer of Grandchildren*, Madeline L'Engle tells the story of bedtime with her grandchildren. At bedtime, her granddaughter Lena turned to her and asked "Is everything all right?" She assured her that things were fine, things were all right. Lena persisted in her question. "Gram, is everything really all right? I mean really?" L'Engle says she "looked at that little child in her white gown and realized that she was asking the cosmic question, the question that is out beyond the safety of this home, full of light and love and warmth." It is the question we ask at Christmas when we come to the manger in Bethlehem and ask "Is everything really all right?" The question occurs again when the glad Easter morning dawns and we gather in record numbers in our churches. The same question is in our hearts: "Is everything really all right?"[5]

It is the reality of the resurrection that gives us a story to proclaim. It is no ordinary story but a redeeming, saving story. If we have heard the story, we must respond. When people come to church they have one great, basic expectation: they want to experience God. It is not an unreasonable expectation but our minds must be focused and our hearts open to the message of hope.

A minister friend of mine was traveling in the south of England when his car broke down. Fortunately, it happened in a little village with a garage so he could get his car repaired. While the mechanics worked on his car, he walked around the village to see what he could learn. As a minister, it was inevitable that he would make his way to the village church. It was an old church and he strolled through the adjacent cemetery. In the corner of the cemetery he noticed a brick wall. The wall enclosed a beautifully maintained rectangle, and he walked over for a closer look. In the enclosed area were fifty graves of young men, ages seventeen to twenty-five. The men were from New Zealand and had died in that village during World War I. Over against the brick wall was a granite marker with the inscription "We shall never forget in this village their sacrifice."[6]

Fifty graves. Why did those young men come so far to die in an English village in 1918? There was no explanation at all. The minster strolled around the village and came to the village museum. He walked in and met the curator who was a volunteer. He asked him to "tell me about the plot in the church cemetery with fifty graves of young soldiers from New Zealand. How did they die and why did they die?" The curator replied "I really don't know, but if you'll give me a day or two I'll see if I can find out." The minister explained that he was having his car repaired and did not know how much longer he would be there and continued to wander around the village asking "Why did they die, and how did they die?" No one in the village really knew. He remembered the marker on the wall in the cemetery: "We shall never forget in this village your sacrifice."

But they *had* forgotten. The village was living a lie. In any life, we can so easily forget the sacrifices that have been made for us.

It is also easy to take Jesus Christ for granted. During a Christmas service this past year, the processional of choirs was assembling in the narthex and there was excitement in the air. As the processional began to move down the center aisle of our sanctuary, my eyes were inevitably drawn to the great Ascension window that dominates the sanctuary. The victorious Christ is before us as we go down the center aisle. Then my eyes dropped just for a moment and rested on the inscription on the pulpit: "The Word Of The Lord Endures Forever." And as we neared the chancel across the front of the communion table: "This do in remembrance of me."

All that we seek to do and accomplish is for him. The church was packed with people who had remembered. There would be no need to remember Christ, or anything else, at Christmas if we had never committed our hearts and lives to him. Why proclaim the gospel if there is no challenge for commitment? He has come, not just to visit us but to occupy our hearts. Has it happened in your life?

For Reflection and Discussion

1. After you have finished this chapter, read Philippians in its entirety. It is a warm-hearted, personal letter from Paul to a congregation and people that he loved deeply. What is its message to us today?

2. After reading the entire book, concentrate with a more detailed and deliberate reading of Chapters 2 and 3. Note particularly 2:5–11 which scholars call "The Christ Hymn." Many believe that this section of Paul's letter was actually sung as a hymn in the early church.

3. What impact should our belief in Christ have on our attitudes (see Philippians 2:14)?

4. What impact should our belief in Christ have on our manner of life (See Philippians 2:15–16)?

5. What do you believe about salvation (see Philippians 3:5–10)?

6. Write down, in fifty words or less, a comprehensive statement of what Christ means to you and share it with your study group.

7. Do you believe that belief in Jesus Christ as Lord and Savior should be a requirement for church membership? Why or why not?

8. We know the sacrifices Christ has made for us. Can you recall the sacrifices, if any, that you have made for him? List five sacrifices you have made for Christ in the order of their magnitude.

9. In most of our churches, there is an inscription on
    the communion table that states "This do in remem-
    brance of me." What does that phrase mean to
    you?

7

Is He Really Alive?

" . . . God will wipe away every tear from their
eyes" (Revelation 7:17, *NRSV*)

Andrew Greeley, a Roman Catholic priest, novelist, and sociologist has observed that we are
born with two realities. First, we have received
the gift of life but we know early on that we will one day
die. Second, we are born with an incurable hope that
death is not the end of us. As Christians, we live with an
eternal hope that "death is swallowed up in the victory" (I
Corinthians 15:54). Our Lord promised that because "I
live, you also will live" (John 14:19). And because of
this, we must face each new day with confidence that
God is with us and with our church, and that during that
day, we will be able to help someone in need. To me,
this is living with a sense of victory. It is resurrection living right now.

Revelation 7:17, our theme verse, is part of a
scene of victory. Those who have suffered in great
tribulation are now gathered before the throne of God in
heaven. The gathering is inclusive, many languages are
spoken, and people of many nations are there. It is a
multiracial gathering and everyone is dressed in white, a
symbol of victory.

A look at the scene as it unfolds reveals three
things about the gathering:

1. They all feel accepted. They have suffered on
   earth but now they are welcomed into the

presence of God. Rejection, isolation, and limitations are now over.

2.   They are joyful. They are singing praise to God
and the vast throng with them are also singing.

3.   They are being rewarded. They are in the presence of God and they are now safe. God is
their shelter and they will never be hungry or
thirsty again. It is in that setting that our theme
verse is given: ". . . and God will wipe away
every tear from their eyes" (Revelation 7:17).

This is one of the most comforting passages in the
Bible. The hymn writer captured the mood of it writing
"the strife is o'er, the battle done, the song of triumph
has already begun. . . ." The central fact of our faith is
the Resurrection. No Resurrection, no New Testament,
no church, no faith, no hope. Without the Resurrection
we have nothing. Without the Resurrection, Jesus of
Nazareth would be a minor footnote on the pages of history. Just a man from the obscure village of Nazareth
who stirred things up a bit, was considered a small
threat to order and peace in the region, and who was
put to death by Roman authorities.

Samuel Shoemaker, the noted Episcopal preacher
from Pittsburgh said "The church and the Bible do not
explain the Resurrection: they are explained by it, and
they start with it. There would be no church and no
Bible unless there had first been the fact of the
Resurrection . . . it is an event of the same order as
Creation itself for it inaugurates a new Creation."[1]

The Freedom of the Resurrection

When we proclaim the gospel, the Resurrection means
that we are safe forever. But safe from what?

1.   Safe from death. Paul said that "death is swallowed up in the victory of our Lord Jesus
Christ" (I Corinthians 15:54). Death no longer
has the final claim on you, on me, or on any of
our loved ones. As I was writing a sermon on

the Resurrection during the summer of 1996, the phone rang and my niece told me that her mother, my only sister, had suddenly died. My first thought, since we had recently lost our brother after a long and agonizing illness, was to thank God that there was no prolonged ordeal of pain and suffering. My second thought was that she was safe. She had had a long and difficult life in many ways but now all of her struggles were over and she was safe.

It is appropriate that we remember our loved ones with gratitude: gratitude for moments shared, services rendered, and the joy of their companionship.

2. Safe from crippling grief. "Safe" does not mean that those left behind are immune from the pain of grief. Death leaves us staggering and in shock. It takes a year or more to work through it and for some, it takes longer. Those who have faith and hope about the eternal can be comforted by the observation often attributed to the late Reverend Dr. Peter Marshall who said " . . . if our loved ones go on to be with God, and He is always with us, then we cannot be far apart!" Wherever we are, those we have loved and lost for a little while are still with us in our memories. Our memories, which are painful at first, in time come to be a source of strength. To remember is really a form of visiting. As long as we can remember shared moments of joy, of meaning, and even of challenge, they are still alive.

One of the ways we prepare for death is to celebrate life. This is the key to being "alive" as long as we live. Christians have an advantage because we know that our living now is in preparation for a larger life to come. We also know that when our loved ones leave us for awhile, there is not only the prospect of a reunion with them but also enlarged life for them, set free from the limitations of this life and often the burdens of infirmities that both cripple and limit. One of the things that will help us in our grieving is to genuinely celebrate the life of the one we have lost.

Terency Elwyn Johnson of Margate Community Church in New Jersey tells the story of Bonnee Hoy, a gifted composer who died at a young age. At the memorial service, a friend spoke about her in loving and revealing ways. A mockingbird used to sing regularly outside Bonnee's window on summer nights. Bonnee would stand at her window and listen, marveling at the beauty of the mockingbird's song. Being a musician, on an impulse one evening, Bonnee decided to sing back. She whistled the first four famous notes of Beethoven's Fifth Symphony. The mockingbird almost immediately sang the notes back and in perfect pitch.

The welcomed mockingbird was absent from time to time and then disappeared for a long period. Then one night, toward the end of Bonnee Hoy's life, the bird returned. In the midst of several of its songs, the mockingbird sang the signature four notes of Beethoven's Fifth. Bonnee's friend, speaking about her at the memorial service, said "I like to think of that now. Somewhere out there is a mockingbird who sings Beethoven because of Bonnee."[2]

3. Safe from the loss of hope. Despair grips our society and crosses all lines: rich and poor, all races, creeds, and circumstance. Musicians have set our despair to music and we hear the jarring notes of their efforts. We see the despair in much of our art and in our media. Many of us are still trying to fully fathom the 1997 Heaven's Gate mass suicide. Christianity does not call us into such cultic isolation. Instead, it calls us to a communion of loving, caring, and service, a community of believers that is always reaching out to the world and trying to make it a better place for us all. Mass suicide is less than God's will for our lives. Those who have the strongest faith in the world to come are those who work the hard-

est, and often the longest, for the world that is the present. The despair around us affords us an opportunity to be the church of proclamation, not only by what we say, but also by what we are. We can be proclaimers of hope by our words and by our living. As Christians, we face life with a point of view of hope.

In a small church in Los Angeles, a sexton saw himself as a shepherd. He took an interest in those who came to the church to pray during the day. His job was church upkeep or maintenance, but he was interested in the "upkeep" of people as well. One man in particular attracted his attention. He would walk into the church just after noon, walk down the center aisle, stand at the chancel steps for a moment, then move on.

The sexton observed this behavior for a few days and began to be concerned about the man. He was not well dressed, he could have used a good bath, and his walk was not steady. The sexton talked to the pastor who suggested he ask the man if there was some way the church could be of help. The man said "No, thank you. I just come in every day and stand before the altar and say 'Jesus, it's Jim.' It is not much of a prayer, but I think God knows what I mean."

Some months went by, and one day the church got a call from the Mother Superior of a home for aged men. The pastor of the church relates the rest of the story: "The Mother Superior told me that Jim had been admitted to the home and I promised to get out to see him. She met me at the door and said that he had been there for two months. He went into the most cantankerous ward we have. Every nun here has tried to bring some kind of joy and calm to that ward. We failed. Jim went into that ward and the place is transformed. It is a new place. I went to him two days ago and asked 'Jim, how is it that you have been able to bring such joy and such a sense of peace to these men?' He said, 'Oh, sister, it is because of my visitor.'[3]

The Mother Superior said that she knew Jim had not had a single visitor in the sixty days he had been there. So she asked Jim what visitor had come to see him. He said 'Sister, every day at 12:00, He comes and stands at the foot of my bed' and says 'Jim, it's Jesus.'"[4]

The continuing reality that Jesus lives empowers us in our lives and in our work. If Jesus lives in you and in me, our lives will reflect that reality. Who we are and what we are will shine through in all that we do. It is the most basic proclamation of the gospel of Jesus Christ that is available to each of us. The Resurrection begins for all of us who are Christians today and it continues forever. Resurrection living is not something that is to be trotted out on Easter Sunday; it is something that should be obvious in our lives every day.

The era of the Iron Curtain and the Cold War were times of darkness that lasted forty-five years. The Berlin Wall, a scar that crossed Germany, divided it, separating family and friends. In Eastern Europe, the church had to go underground. Its members mounted a silent witness under persecution but its witness was actually anything but silent. It went underground but still held on to the light of hope in dark circumstances. Christians worked and prayed, read their Bibles, baptized their babies, and many continued to go to church which caused great hardship.

When the Iron Curtain came down and the Berlin Wall fell, we discovered a church that was fervent and alive. One of the most dramatic moments of this period occurred in Czechoslovakia in November of 1989. A group of students was confronted by a cadre of soldiers and out of that event, a shock wave traveled across the nation. Christians decided that at noon on November 18, 1989, everyone in the country would walk out of their homes, away from their businesses, put down their tools at their jobs, and walk into the streets. Church bells in Czechoslovakia that had not rung for forty-five years tolled, and on that particular day, the streets were jammed with people demanding freedom. The church bells continued to ring all day long, and pastors of churches long prohibited from posting any public notices or messages, nailed a simple message on their church doors which read "The Lamb Has Won."[5]

What a gospel we have to proclaim: "The Lamb Has Won." He lives, he has conquered death. The essential question is does he live in you and in me?

The poet Ann Weems has endeared herself to Presbyterians. In her wonderful book, *Kneeling in Jerusalem*, she has penned these lines:

> The silence breaks into morning
> The one star lights the world.
> The lily springs to life.
>
> Let it begin with singing
> and never end!
> Angels, quit your lamenting!
> And pilgrims,
> upon your knees in tearful prayers,
> rise up, and take your hearts
> and run!
>
> We who were no people
> are named anew
> God's people,
> for he who was no more
> is now alive forevermore.[6]

Does he live in you?

For Reflection and Discussion

1. Is the Resurrection the centerpiece of your faith?
2. What has it meant in your church and your community to be "resurrection people?"
3. Resurrection means new life. Do you sense that your church is encouraging that new life?
4. Does Christ live in you?

8

We Worship Regularly

"As His custom was, He (Jesus) went into the synagogue on the Sabbath day, and stood up to read." (Luke 4:16)

William Temple, Former Archbishop of Canterbury, has defined worship in its essence and in its power: "Worship is the submission of all our nature to God. It is the quickening of our conscience by his holiness; the nourishment of the mind with his truth; the purifying of imagination by his beauty; the opening of the heart to his love, the surrender of his will to his purpose—and all gathered up in adoration, the most selfless emotion of which nature is capable and therefore, the chief remedy for that self-centeredness, which is our original sin and the source of all actual sin."[1]

From this, we recognize that worship is

the heart of the church's life

our best opportunity to be evangelical, pastoral, educational, and prophetic

the place where the tone of a church is set, where the vision is shared, and where people are prepared to go out and proclaim the gospel

an activity involving all the people, clergy, and laity

Worship is a dynamic act, not a passive observation. That has been recognized by many, including

Annie Dillard who said about worship "It is madness to wear ladies' straw hats to church . . . we should be wearing crash helmets. Ushers should issue life preservers and signal flares; they should lash us to our pews . . . God may draw us out to where we can never return."[2]

When they attend worship, people's one great desire is to experience God. Things can and do happen in worship when the mind is open, the heart is seeking, and the spirit is expectant. We should approach our participation in worship with expectancy. Worship should invite us to draw closer to Christ. The worship should challenge us to examine where we are and to be open to where God might want us to be. It should be joyous and celebrative, contemplative, and challenging. We should prepare ourselves for worship and pray for others who will be seated around us. It is our best opportunity to collectively proclaim the gospel of salvation. When worship is over, everyone should leave with new resolve to engage the world about us for Christ because together, we have been in the presence of God.

Perhaps there should be an inscription over the doors of every sanctuary in our nation that states "All who enter here are participants in worship. Are you prepared? For God awaits." Our basic attitude should not be "what can the preacher do for me today?", "Will the choir be on or off today?", "I wonder who I'll see in church today?" or "I hope there is some good reading in the church bulletin during the preliminaries."

Our theme verse tells us that worship was the steady habit of Jesus: "as was his custom." We notice that immediately after his temptations in the desert, he went home to worship.

The Gifts of Worship

When we worship we gain perspective; for while worship is centered on God, it must also touch life in real ways. Russell C. Long has observed that "worship liberates the personality by giving a new perspective to life."

Worship should also bring us peace. It is obvious from the Gospels that Jesus drew strength and peace from his worship. He was reminded that he was under-girded by a strength greater than his own.

Worship also lets us contemplate the issues that matter in life. As Jesus stood to read the lesson in his hometown synagogue, it was clear to him what he was about. He was to peach good news to the poor, heal the broken, release the captives, cause the blind to see, and set at liberty those who were oppressed. He reminded everyone there that God cares and will bless everyone who comes to him (Luke 4:18–19).

A Public Proclamation for God

One of the most effective ways we proclaim the gospel as Christians is the witness of our regular worship. We declare publicly to friends, family, and acquaintances where we stand when we go to worship. One of the greatest parishioners I've known was a man who was hearing impaired; he had only ten percent of his hearing in one ear. I was having lunch with him one day and we talked about worship. I told him how encouraged I was about his regular attendance at worship. I especially appreciated his attendance, knowing that he had severe limitations in hearing both the music and the spoken parts of the service. I will never forget what he said: "I just want everyone to know whose side I'm on." The witness of a church packed with people at worship is a powerful testimony as to what we are and what we believe.

What do you expect to happen when you worship? When our worship team at Peachtree Presbyterian meets, the objective of our planning and prayer is God. We want everyone who worships to feel God's presence, to sense God's nearness, and to experience God's love and strength. We recall and heed some blunt advice from Ecclesiastes 5:1: "As you enter the temple, keep your ears open and your mouth shut."

Our hope and prayer is that our worship will give all who are there a vision of God: a new awareness of his presence and his power and his availability to us by his grace. We also want those who worship with us to reach a verdict about God. Our worship should lead us to some decisions about God. Some will be moved to decide by the music, others by the prayers, still others by the sense of oneness in the gathered community. Others will be brought to a moment of choice by the sermon. But no matter the circumstance, worship should bring us to some convincing moments of choice about God.

All those who plan to participate in worship should be sure that its focus is on God. It is God whom we adore and praise in our worship. Worship, in its focus on God, should also touch life in relevant and revealing ways. God is not ours to manage on a string but is the one interested in our needs. Sara Maitland, feminist, theologian and novelist, reports that her computer spell-check wanted to change the word "sacred" to "scared." We are not to be afraid in the presence of God, but we are also not to be flippant. The proper word to describe what we should feel is awe and in Christian worship, joy, because God loves us. We need, says Maitland, to remind ourselves of God's grandeur and "otherness" as well as God's tenderness and generosity. It is my hope that when we worship, each worshipper will hear and heed the questions that came to Isaiah: "Who will go for us?" Isaiah answered "Lord, I'll go." (Isaiah 6:8)

Worship should raise questions in our minds, essential inquiries such as "Does God know me?", "Do I matter?", and "Does God care about me?" The quick answers are of course God knows us, of course we matter, and we matter because we are his. But these questions have been around a long time. Again and again in the Bible the question is raised "O that I knew where I might find God?" I rather suspect that it is not so much our finding God but God's finding us. God is always searching, looking for you and me. We most often encounter God when we worship. Where we worship is God's place and he has promised that where "two or three are gathered in his name" that he will be with us.

We can, when we worship be surprised by the renewed sense of the presence of God in our worship and in our lives. God knows who we are and desires an encounter with us. We can know God if we seek him.

We are urged to "call upon him when he is near." Getting to know God is a cultivated relationship. But unless we "harden our hearts," we will always have the hunger for God but we will never have a relationship with God unless we cultivate it. It helps to be born into a Christian family, but you cannot inherit a personal faith; you have to come to that commitment yourself.

Several years ago, I asked each member of a confirmation class to write me a personal letter and answer two questions. The first question was "Why do you want to join the church?" Two of the answers I received were unforgettable. One confirmant asserted that "He did not know why he wanted to join the church. It was for that reason that he was in 'this dumb class.'" Another wrote she was ready to join because "Church ran in the family." It is good when church runs in the family but someday, somehow, and the sooner the better, we all must make a decision for ourselves.

When we worship, a question of involvement should be raised in every heart. "Is there something I need to do or to be?" Of course there is. Our experience of worship should not only mobilize the will, but also move the feet to go and to do. There are people and causes for whom our actions can make a decisive difference if we will just get moving. There should be some peak experiences in our worship. We should build on those experiences, not just stand on them. Having the Olympics in Atlanta was a peak experience in the city's history. But what now? How shall we build on that experience? Can we mobilize thousands of volunteers who will, with great joy, join their hearts and their energies to housing the homeless, feeding the hungry, and build here a city that can be set on a hill "whose builder and maker is God?" Are we now, post-Olympics, more open to people of other races and cultures? Are we less parochial?

The most frequently asked question about worship that comes to me is "Why is public worship so important?" If Jesus needed to worship, is there any doubt that we need it as well? A friend of mine said some weeks ago "I feel no need to worship." She meant that she felt no need for public worship. As I noted earlier, many share her feelings and many times I have heard people say "I can worship God everywhere and anywhere."

This sounds true, in theory, for God is everywhere, but is it, in fact, true? The answer is no. It is no because we simply do not do it. Public worship should give us focus on God and cause us to look inward at ourselves. Our worship should cleanse, challenge, convince, and comfort. Private worship feels too much like "the bootstrap fallacy," too much reliance on self and not enough on God.

I suspect that it is a superman/superwoman fallacy of strength and independence that is at the heart of the movement to "private worship." It is totally subjective, focused on self-sufficiency instead of God's grace and goodness. Life will quickly prove to us the inadequacy of such a stance. Beyond this, private worship offers no witness to others. There is something to be said about hundreds of people assembling and lifting heart and voice in praise to God in public worship. It is a powerful witness to God for hundreds of people to get off buses or park their cars and move toward the sanctuary to worship. Those driving by have a visible public witness that God matters.

I think that if any church were filled to capacity but not a word was uttered or a sound was heard, all of us there would be helped nonetheless. I believe that, because if we are there together, we are focusing our thoughts on God. If we listened for the voice of God to speak to us, it would help us. It would reinforce us because of the power of our being there together in the presence of God. It would remind us that we are not alone when we worship. God is there and others are there. Those who hurt, those who are lonely, those who are afraid, and some who want to shout their joy—all are there together in the presence of God. Public worship is essential; it is crucial. We need, our souls need, and our hearts need the evaluation and inspiration of worship.

Our need for worship is greater than God's need for us *to* worship. God is like a shepherd who leads his flock to a place where nourishing food is abundant but God does not make us eat. God provides for us, but God does not force feed. If we are to respond to the challenge and opportunity of proclaiming the gospel for the salvation of humankind, we must accept God's hospitality and become a worshipping church. Those who proclaim must have heard and responded to the gospel. Those who are seekers must be invited to participate in worship where the gospel is taught. They must be able to observe around them persons who are living out the gospel that they have heard in their lives.

During the reign of Oliver Cromwell, the British government ran short of silver coins. Lord Cromwell sent his men to a local cathedral to see if they could find any precious metals. They came back with an encouraging report: we have found silver in the statues of the saints standing in the corner of the cathedral. Cromwell, the soldier statesman, issued a blunt order: "Good! We'll melt down the saints and put them in circulation."[3]

What a great thought! We do need to "melt down the saints'" and get them circulating; active, out where the people are; out where the seekers are eager to be found. Ann Weems has words that inspire:

> "O Amazing God, you come into our
>   ordinary lives
> and set a holy table among us,
> Filing our plates with the Bread of Life
> and our cups with salvation.
> Send us out, O God,
> with tender heartedness
> To touch an ordinary everyday world
> with the promise of your holiness."[4]

For Reflection and Discussion

1. Is worship the heart of your church's life?
2. How do you prepare for worship?
3. Do you let your children, after they attend Sunday school, sit with you in worship?

4. How often do you worship? Once a week? Once a month? Only at Christmas and Easter?

5. Does your church encourage children to participate in worship?

9

Faith—Conviction or Convenience?

"Why were you so fearful? Don't you even yet have confidence in me?" (Mark 4:40)

We proclaim the gospel for salvation because we believe that people can be changed. Kathryn Lindskoog started an article on C. S. Lewis' *Search For Joy* with two quotations. One is from Lewis, the other is from Karl Marx, both of whom were seventeen at the time. One of the quotations talks about joy, the other does not. These are the quotations:

> "Union with Christ imparts an inner elevation, comfort in affiliations, tranquil reliance, and a heart which opens itself to everything noble and great, not for the sake of ambition or desire for fame, but for the sake of Christ. Union with Christ produces joy . . . it is joy known only to the simple and childlike heart, united with Christ and through him with God, a joy which elevates life and makes it more beautiful."[1]

> "You know, I think that I believe in no religion. There is absolutely no proof for any of them, and from a philosophical standpoint, Christianity is not even the best. All religions, that is, all mythologies to give them their proper name, are merely man's invention . . . primitive man found himself surrounded by all sorts of terrible things he didn't understand . . . thus religion, that is to say, mythology, grew up. Often, too,

great men were regarded as gods after their
death—such as Hercules . . . Christianity came
into being, one mythology among many . . . I
am not laying down as a certainty that there is
nothing outside the material world . . . anything
may exist."[2]

As Kathryn Lindskoog notes in her article, both of the
quotations above were made when C. S. Lewis and Karl
Marx were very young and not really as settled in their beliefs as they sound. Our immediate question is "What happened?" It is obvious that Marx regressed and lost his faith.
It is also obvious that C. S. Lewis found a relationship to
Christ that was real. Some respond to the proclamation of
the gospel and come to faith; some do not respond. It is
our responsibility to proclaim the faith. Those who hear it
have the responsibility of an appropriate response.

Even in the close circle of disciples around Jesus,
some responded deeply, others struggled. The Bible
says that as the ministry of our Lord unfolded, the common people "heard him gladly" (Mark 12:37). There was
an authenticity about him and his words had the ring of
truth. His teachings connected with things that were real.
He could take an illustration from the familiar—"consider
the lilies of the field"—or note the fall of a sparrow and
turn it into a comforting thought or a challenging concept.
The press of people was so great that from time to time
he had to get away for some rest. The theme verse of
this chapter comes out of such an event.

Mark tells the story of Jesus and his Disciples cross-
ing the Sea of Galilee and being caught in a sudden,
dangerous, alarming storm. Once in the boat, Jesus
went to sleep but suddenly there was danger. The boat
was about to be swamped. Sudden storms on the Sea
of Galilee were not unusual This small body of water is
surrounded by a ring of mountains. The winds come
down through the mountain passes in a type of tunnel-
ing effect and smooth sailing can suddenly become
dangerous as the winds hit the surface of the sea.

The Disciples, fearing that the boat was about to
capsize, waked Jesus up saying "Teacher, don't you

even care that we are all about to drown" (Mark 4:38)?
They were obviously very afraid. They had seen him
care for people in all kinds of ways and conditions.
They needed help, and they needed it now; and it was
in that context of fear that our theme verse is given "Why
were you so fearful? Don't you even yet have confidence in me" (Mark 4:40)?

Our faith ought to have the capacity to steady us
whatever the challenge but sometimes it does not. Our
faith should give us confidence and peace whatever
the circumstances but sometimes it does not. All of us
have to raise the essential questions about life and
faith as we grow in our relationship to Christ. It is easy
to have great faith when the sun is shining but when
the storms of life assail us, it is often a different matter.
Faith in Christ should be a steadying conviction, not a
convenience trotted out in an emergency. Often, we
develop a working premise in our relationship to God.
It goes something like this: Lord, if you will help me
with the really big things in life, I personally will take
care of all of the minor matters that come up in the
daily routine!

It sounds plausible, even reasonable. But it will not
work because in matters small we set the tone of where
we place our trust. If, as a matter of daily routine, we
place our trust in ourselves, then we are going to have
trouble when a tragedy engulfs us. The writer of
Hebrews defines faith as "The evidence of things not
seen" (Hebrews 11:1). It is the capacity to hold on, to
keep steady, to have an underlying trust in God even
when the way ahead is not clear or the issues involved
are beyond our understanding and grasp. The Disciples
in the tossing boat, in their fear, raised a basic question:
"Don't you even care about us" (Mark 4:38)?

When a tragedy has occurred, one of the first issues raised is the question of God's care. How could
God let this happen? What have we done to displease
God? The mind cannot grasp the tragic reality and the
heart refuses to accept it. Therefore, we can easily conclude that God does not really notice or care what is
happening to us.

If God is attentive, why does he allow some things to happen? Is God incapable or unwilling? Our human experiences cause us to doubt and some of them drive us to despair.

I am indebted to Dr. Lewis Thomas, the physician, who for many years headed The Sloan Kettering Cancer Center and who was also a gifted writer for his insights on "the gift of ambiguity." Much of God's light shines in darkness, he noted. There is enough darkness in each of our lives to cause us to wonder what, in God's name, is going on. Yet we would have to affirm that there is enough light and assurance to enable us to trust even when we cannot grasp what a particular event means.

Matthew's version of the storm on the Sea of Galilee has Jesus coming to the rocking boat in the 'fourth watch of the night' (Matthew 14:25). It was the darkest hour of the night and he came. It is that reality to which our faith clings in the dark hours. We are convinced that he cares and that he will come to stand with us. We can only trust in God even when we do not fully understand. It is not easy; it never has been; it never will be.

Challenges and Doubt

The challenges that confront us cause us to doubt. When we doubt, we are in good company. Isaiah the Prophet said "Truly, thou are a God who hides thyself" (Isaiah 45:15). Job, who bore much suffering, cried out "If only I knew where to find him; if only I could go to his dwelling! I would state my case before him and fill my mouth with arguments. I would find out what he would answer me, and consider what he would say. Would he oppose me with great power? No, he would not press charges against me. There an upright man could present his case before him, and I would be delivered forever from my judge. But if I go to the east, he is not there; if I go to the west, I do not find him. When he is at work in the north, I do not see him; when he turns to the south, I catch no glimpse of him. But he knows the way that I take; when he has tested me, I will come forth as gold. My feet have closely followed his steps; I have kept to his way without turning aside I have not departed from the commands of his lips; I have treasured the words of his mouth more than my daily bread. But he stands alone, and who can oppose him? He does whatever he pleases. He carries out his decree against me, and many such plans he still has in store. That is why I am terrified before him; when I think of all this, I fear him, God has made my heart faint; the Almighty has terrified me. Yet I am not silenced by the darkness, by the thick darkness that covers my face" (Job 23:3–17).

We've all been there, haven't we? And if you haven't, you will be. We must, on a daily basis, cultivate our faith so that when the challenges come, we will have the framework for strength and hope as Job did. An old Scottish proverb says "I thatched my roof when the weather was dry." It is wise advice. We prepare for the rainy days when the sun is shining. We will find, as the bumper sticker affirms, that "Grace Happens" if we are living and trusting each day. Moving from the moment of faith's conviction, when we have responded in our own hearts to the proclamation of the gospel, we should come to that moment when we can trust and hope in the darkest of days. When William Butler Yeats died, his friend W. H. Auden wrote "In the desert of the heart, let the healing fountain start to flow."

It can happen, and will happen, if we are living our lives in the context of a larger trust in God. If our faith is a mere convenience, it is something that we trot out when times are good, when life's challenges are manageable. If it is a conviction, it is a way of life in matters large and small.

There are three elements to faith as conviction. First, we must trust in God. We are to put all of our "religious eggs" in one basket. Instead, we often put our faith in the strangest things. Sometimes it is because we are desperate; at other times it is because we have a spiritual energy that needs expression and we express it in unusual ways. Some people cannot start their day without reading their horoscope. When life falls in, your horoscope is not going to help you very much.

We sometimes make the mistake of putting the faith in ourselves. Faith in God must be the foundation of our living. If our basic faith decision is up for grabs every morning, then it will not be adequate for life. Mother Teresa acknowledged this every day by her actions, saying "I knew that if the world belonged to me, it would die with me." Her faith and trust were not in herself. She trusted in God.

And if faith is to be a conviction, it must be more than intellectual pursuit. It must become heartfelt reality. It is as the Bible says: ". . . the substance of things hoped for, the evidence of things not seen" (Hebrews 11:1 *New King James Version*).

We cannot see it but we, nonetheless, know, sense, and feel that it is true. In that boat, on a stormy sea, water splashing over the side into the boat, the darkness about them, "the wind against them" (Matthew 14:24), all the Disciples had was faith; and it was centered in Christ.

When faith is a conviction; it is real in any kind of weather. It undergirds our joy when we celebrate and it keeps us steadfast when storms challenge. I have always liked what Leonard Griffith said about a faith that sustains: "Christianity is always at its best when the world is at its worse. It is at its best intellectually when the world is confused . . . it is at its best morally when men (and women) have lost their values and their standards . . . it is at its best socially when men (and women) are . . . at each other's throats . . . it is at its best spiritually when men (and women) have lost the sense of the presence of God."[3]

Faith as conviction is a growing faith. One of the things church is all about is that it is a nourishing community.

Picasso painted Gertrude Stein when she was young and again as an older woman of maturity and wisdom. She was no longer tentative in the portrait. People were startled and said to Picasso "That doesn't look like her." Picasso replied "Oh, I know, but she will one day look just like that!"[4] We must have a vision of our unrealized future and capacity for growth. Our objective is to have a mature faith. I have that vision for all men and women of faith. It does not yet appear what we shall be but if we keep the faith, keep trusting in God, and keep growing, one day we will have a faith that will stand us steady when the storms come. And they will come. Faith that is a conviction is a growing faith that is centered in the one whom we proclaim as Jesus Christ.

The Confessions of St. Augustine reveal a man who struggled in his inner life between faith and human desire. Yet through the prayers of his mother and his own searching, he came to know that all of our hearts are restless until we find our roots in God. I was moved one morning as I read the following passage from his *Confessions*: "As the time comes when you no longer wish to see, O God, what I previously desired when instead your will is what you wanted it is then that you purify me. But where has my freedom been for so long? From what secret depths was it dragged out in an instant that I might agree now to bow my head beneath your yoke which is gentle and accept on my shoulders your burden which is light, O Lord Jesus Christ my strength and my redeemer? How suddenly and comforting it was to lose the false comforts of the past! I had long feared losing them, and now it was a joy to cast them away. Truly it was you who put them far from me, my true and supreme comfort; You put them far away and set yourself in their place in my heart."⁵

Faith is a conviction, when, and only when, we put our trust finally, fully, and completely in Jesus Christ. You cannot proclaim a faith you don't have!

For Reflection and Discussion

1. Is yours a growing faith?
2. What challenges have you experienced of late that tested your faith?
3. The disciplines of a growing faith are prayer, Bible study worship, and fellowship with other Christians. How do you measure your faith by those disciplines?
4. Do you consider doubt a good test for faith? How do you answer your doubts?
5. List five challenges to your faith of the past year.

PART III
The Response

10

I Want to Proclaim the Gospel but I Need Help

"What is the Holy Spirit? (Acts 19:2—*The Living Bible*)

Years ago, an American pastor visited Charles Spurgeon's church in London. The visitor noted that there was little heat in the sanctuary. He inquired of Spurgeon whether or not the church had a heating plant. He was led to the basement of the church by the distinguished minister and they entered a large room, Spurgeon then explained that before every service, 400 members met in that room to pray for their pastor and the salvation of the lost. Then he turned to the visitor and said "This is the church's real heating plant!"

The early church service was launched by a prayer meeting in a room where the Disciples were waiting as Jesus had instructed them. The Disciples were vastly different after they had been convinced of the Resurrection of Jesus Christ and empowered by the Holy Spirit. This vacillating, ambivalent group who fled the city after Jesus' arrest—once all of them but one were convinced and empowered by the Spirit—were martyred for their witness. They literally proclaimed the gospel to the known world of their day through this empowerment.

The theme verse of this chapter asks a very relevant question: "*What* is the Holy Spirit?" Perhaps a more pointed question would be "*Who* is the Holy Spirit?" When that question is asked, we immediately react because we associate the Holy Spirit with excessive exuberance in religious expression. We hear about "speaking in tongues" or "healing services" and generally, we are uncomfortable with the discussion.

The Holy Spirit is one expression of how God has revealed himself. We believe in a triune God: Father, Son, and Holy Spirit. This does not mean that we believe in "three gods." God has made himself known to us in three distinctive ways. Maxie Dunnam, President of Asbury Seminary, has said that what we are talking about is "God for us, God with us, and God in us."[1] I have always been helped in my own thinking to think of the Holy Spirit as God in the present tense.

As we seek to proclaim the gospel to others, inevitably, at some point, people will ask questions about the Holy Spirit. It has been helpful to me to share my thoughts on the Holy Spirit in this way. In the Old Testament, God was remote and seemed almost unapproachable. In the dawning of the New Testament, God drew near to us, walked among us, lived as we live, suffered as we suffer, and died as we die. We see the full heart of God revealed in his Son, our Savior Jesus Christ. After the death and Resurrection of Jesus Christ who "ascended into heaven," there was the coming of the Holy Spirit: God with us, God in the present tense. We are, therefore, empowered by his Spirit to do his work today.

For Christians, God has fully disclosed himself in Jesus Christ. He has enabled the Holy Spirit to empower the church and its people. The Holy Spirit has one function: to make real in your heart and mind the teachings of Jesus Christ. When we sit down with a person to share our faith journey, it is right and proper that we ask God to direct us by his Spirit so that our words will be God's and the heart of the person with whom we are conversing will be open. As the teachings of Christ are made real to us and to others, we are often convinced, sometimes converted, almost always channeled and, if our hearts are opened, always changed. All of that is the work of the Holy Spirit making real to us and through us the teachings of Jesus Christ.

The presence of the Holy Spirit is not passive but active and empowering. The Spirit turns doubters into believers, makes the timid bold in their witness, and causes the weak to be strong. We are also given new power to overcome "brokenness" in our lives, to cope with things with which we have to struggle every day, and the inner urging to repent our sins. But the essential task of the Holy Spirit is to make real, in your life and mine, the teachings of Jesus Christ.

Recognizing the Holy Spirit

How are we to know the Holy Spirit? People occasionally share with me, as a minister, messages or spiritual insights from God. They believe they have received a message from the Holy Spirit. I listen and then I test what people are saying to me by one simple reality: Is this message consistent and in harmony with the teachings of Jesus Christ? If it is, then one should listen. If it is not, then it is not from the Holy Spirit.

Writer Doug Murren has provided a checklist of spiritual experiences that enables us to discern the presence of the Holy Spirit in our actions and experiences:

1. Has this spiritual gift or experience taken your will from you? If so, it is not of God (I Corinthians 14:1–5).

2. Has it brought you peace? Is it peaceful? Is the experience understandable to other spiritual people? If not, it may not be authentic (James 3:13–18).

3. Has this experience glorified God? Is Jesus the center of your experience or are you the center? The Bible makes clear that in the movement of the Holy Spirit, Jesus Christ is at the center. All biblically sound spiritual experiences are Christ centered (I Corinthians 12:1–3; John 14–16).

4. Did the experience enhance your respect for others or did it cause you to feel superior? If it caused you to feel superior to others, it may not be of God (I Corinthians 14: 1–5).

5. Are you willing to share the expression of your experience with your pastor and test it by his or her experience? If not, why? Be careful that it may not be a true experience.

6. Has your experience or insight strengthened your relationship to Christ, to his church, and the foundational doctrines of the faith? No true experience will take you to extremes or violate basic doctrine (Deuteronomy 18: 9–22).

7. Has your experience caused you to be more concerned for others? If so, this experience is producing the right kind of fruit that is both biblical and legitimate (I Corinthians 12–14).

8. Has this experience caused you to walk in a closer harmony with Jesus Christ? If you are experiencing feelings of superiority and isolation, it may not be valid (I Corinthians 12).

9. Is your experience open to anyone? Can you share it? If you feel that it is yours and yours alone, it is probably not a legitimate or genuine experience. If it is true to Christ, then it is to be shared with others (Acts 10:34–36).[2]

The Holy Spirit gives us clear, constant direction that is consistent with the teachings of Christ. When you think of his teaching, it is never self-centered but reaches out to others. He does not teach superiority but humility. His teaching does not produce division; it produces love. He said "all will know that you are my disciples if you have love for one another" (John 13:35). People who have had dramatic experiences of the Spirit of God must avoid spiritual pride that reflects a sense of superiority.

Such an attitude is not the attitude of Jesus Christ who accepted people where they were in their spiritual and life journey and caused them to grow. One of the great challenges in the church is to keep "the spiritual eagles" from killing "the baby birds." If we are not careful, the "spiritual eagles" will think of "the baby birds" as lazy young louts who are not serious about their faith. This sets up a counter reaction as "the baby birds" see "the spiritual eagles" as wild-eyed fanatics who have too much religion and have become pushy, rigid, and unbending.

We are all in need of appropriate direction from the Holy Spirit. And we need a deeper understanding of the teachings of Jesus Christ. If, with humility and openness, we are eager to learn from each other, then there is a healthy way in which the spiritually mature can assist and learn from the eager openness of "the baby birds." I have always loved the story that Bishop Fulton J. Sheen told. He was scheduled to speak in Philadelphia. He was not familiar with the city and became hopelessly lost as he tried to find the City Hall. He noticed some young people talking together and asked them for directions. One of the kids asked him what he was going to do at City Hall. He replied "I am going to give a lecture." They asked "About what?" He told them that he was lecturing on "How to get to heaven" and invited them to come along and hear his lecture. They responded "Are you kidding? You don't even know how to get to City Hall!"[3]

There is something healthy and honest about the exchange between the famous bishop and the kids on the street. All of us, bishops included, need direction. The Spirit of God can give us direction and the direction of the Spirit is always in keeping with the teachings of Christ.

If I seem to belabor the point, it is because I see so many excesses in this area. We often attribute events to the Holy Spirit that are simply not true. The Bible says that the Holy Spirit is like the wind; it comes and goes and we never know from whence it came or where it is going. The only thing we know for sure is that it will be moving us in a direction consistent with the teachings of Jesus Christ.

There are two things that can be said with certainty about the Holy Spirit.

First, the Holy Spirit is not anyone's personal possession. We easily forget that God's ways are not our ways and God's thoughts are not our thoughts. For example, a friend arrived at a conference center. He was attending a seminar and his hostess greeted him with these words: "I now know who the Holy Spirit has placed at table number seven!"

The Holy Spirit leads and guides us as we pray and as we proclaim the gospel. This guidance is always in keeping with the teachings of Christ, but given the range of things that capture the attention of God, it is hard to visualize that who sits at table seven at a mountain conference center is a high priority. Would it not trouble you to know that the Holy Spirit was preoccupied with place cards at table seven when a teenager is killed in a drive-by shooting on the streets of Atlanta? Table place cards and drive-by shootings are rooted in human choice. The death of a teenager brings sorrow to the heart of God and to us all. We need the Holy Spirit's comfort and guidance as we seek to grapple with the cycles of deprivation that fuel such anger and chaos.

Second, the Spirit does not indulge us in endless experiences of pious ecstasy. The kind of opious ecstasy that some claim in their spiritual experience, attributed to the Holy Spirit, becomes, if we are not careful, a spiritual narcotic. We do not have to be saved at every revival. Every worship service might not provide a spiritual high. Our worship provides spiritual nourishment, comfort, strength, guidance, and peace. Worship, under the leadership of the Holy Spirit, will challenge some, convince others, and hopefully clarify spiritual issues and deepen all of us in our relationship with Jesus Christ. We should be inspired and motivated as we worship to share our story about our journey with Christ with others. This is the most basic way we proclaim the gospel. The Spirit empowers the people of God to share our journey with others. The gospel that most people know and experience is what they see of Christ in us and through us.

Some persons never get beyond the beginning in their faith experience. They may come to know, in a moment of intense personal belief, guided by the Holy Spirit. This is all right. It does not mean that the experience has to come again and again. There is a point of "beginning" only once.

Many young Christians drop out of the church or by the wayside because they are unable to move beyond the point of beginning. It is important that when our point of beginning is real, that we then move on and be nurtured and cultivated in our faith. We must begin to practice the basic disciplines of worship, Bible study, prayer, Christian service, and all of the things that help us grow in spiritual ways. Our faith is lived out in the community of believers, the church. Our churches must be nourishing communities that are moving us to spiritual maturity. The new believer will fall by the wayside or out of the church if he or she is not encouraged by others to grow.

The Holy Spirit is present when we engage in the study of our Bibles; present when we open our hearts and minds in worship and prayer; and present when we join hands with others in Christian service. All of the daily things we do to cultivate our faith finds the Spirit present to guide and to strengthen. The daily disciplines are as important as the mountaintop experiences. No one can stay on the mountaintop forever, for there is work to be done for Christ in the valleys of opportunity where we live and work. Real faith must be practiced and lived out in a real world.

The experiences that cause us to grow are as varied as we are individuals. One of the most exciting things we are doing at Peachtree Presbyterian is building houses with Habitat for Humanity. We have now built seventy homes toward a goal of one hundred. Everything that happens on a site where a home is being built is good. New friendships are made. The group of people gathered, while intergenerational, is usually weighted toward those in their twenties. But you have "mature" Christians interacting and involved with "young Christians" and with some who have never made a profession of faith. Building houses for the homeless is one of the ways we can proclaim the gospel. Best of all, while the building process is going on, the builders get to know the family that will occupy the house. Friendships develop as walls are painted, foundations are laid, roofing is nailed down, and appliances are installed.

At the end of the day, tired builders and joyous homeowners to be view the work of their hands and their hearts. They see that where once there was just a hole, a foundation is now set and the framework of a house visible. They can see what they have done together. One young man who had been on-site building for several weeks came to see me. He could not talk about the experience without tears, nor could I listen without tears. At the end of our visit he said "'I am now ready to make a profession of faith in Jesus Christ and join the church. By the way, I'll need to be baptized!"

Most of the time, most of us experience the Holy Spirit in ordinary places. All of us need some mountaintop experience to sustain and inspire us. The young man who found Christ while building a home for a homeless family had a mountaintop experience that led him to Christ. Now that he has been baptized, he is still building houses for the homeless but he is also sharing his journey with others. He is regular in worship, has found a small Bible study group, and is involved in a Sunday school class. The Spirit is guiding him in all of these things as he grows and matures.

A famous evangelist named Dwight L. Moody was visiting one day with a Chicago businessman. Moody was talking with the man about his faith but was told by the businessman that he simply did not have time for it, and really didn't think he needed to participate in the church. Moody did not argue with him but simply got up and walked to the fireplace. He paused before the warming fire, took a pair of fire tongs in hand, and lifted a blazing, burning, red hot coal from the fire. He placed it on the hearth and went back to his chair. He did not say a word and the two men sat there lost in their own thoughts, watching the blazing, red hot coal on the hearth. The coal, separated from the fire, began to fade, to lose its glow. It smoldered, turned dark, and went out. The blazing coal had died and soon it was cold. It had lost its heat. The man to whom Moody had been talking turned to the evangelist and said "I understand."[4]

None of us will make it in our faith journey without the fellowship and nurture of other Christians. The church can and does provide a nurturing environment where we help and reinforce one another.

The world around us, the seekers who come to experience who we are in the church, want to see the work of God through us and in us. We often forget that we should be letting our light shine for Christ before the world.

In the summer of 1805, a number of native-American chiefs met at Buffalo Creek in New York. They heard a sermon by a Mr. Cram from the Boston Missionary Society. When he had concluded his sermon, he gave the invitation to discipleship. One of the chiefs, Red Jacket, stood up and said to Mr. Cram: "Brother, we are told that you have been preaching to white people in this place. These people have become our neighbors. We are acquainted with them. We will wait a little while to see what effect your preaching has upon them. If we find it does them good, makes them honest and less disposed to cheat Indians, we will then consider again what you have said to us today about your Christ."[5]

The world around us today is saying to the church and its people that "we hear what you are saying," we will now watch how you live out what you profess. The world has every right to want to see how God is at work in us by his Spirit before they seriously consider how God might work in them. When we sit in our churches for worship, we are the church gathered to receive our marching orders. When the worship is over and our service begins, we become the church scattered to do the work of Christ in the world. Our faith is to be lived every day, whether we are at home, at work, or at play.

The Gifts of the Holy Spirit

One of the greatest challenges in the Bible concerning our faith journey is that "by their fruits ye shall know them." Paul, in Galatians 5:22, tells us that there are nine fruits divided into three groups:

> 1. Three of the fruits of the Spirit are gifts of God and include love, joy, and peace.

2. Three of the fruits reveal who we are, qualities that should emanate from your life and mine. These qualities are long-suffering, kindness, and goodness.

3. Three of the fruits of the Spirit are rooted in human choice: they are faithfulness, gentleness, and self-control.

The gifts that God gives us by his Spirit are "love, joy, and peace" (Galatians 5:22). We love because he first loved us. Our human capacity for love is enhanced by the reality of God's love for us, and in our response to his love. We are filled with joy as Christians because we are the objects of someone's love, especially the love of God as seen in Christ. When we experience both love and joy, it should bring us a sense of peace. Peace is not just the cessation of hostilities or the absence of strife, both of which are good and desirable; instead, peace represents a sense of wholeness and harmony in our lives. Implicit in this kind of peace is that our relationship to God and to others is unimpaired.[6]

Then there are those gifts of the Spirit that should be revealed in our living—long-suffering, gentlemness, and kindness. Someone has observed that kindness is the music that even the deaf can hear. Do you remember when Ohio State University football Coach Woody Hayes hit a Clemson player? His action ended his career as a coach. The same year, a sports banquet was held for the NFL players. Tom Landry, Head Coach of the Dallas Cowboys, was one of the principal speakers. The speakers were allowed to bring one guest and Landry invited Woody Hayes. It was an act of kindness. Surely the working of the Spirit of God in us will proclaim that we belong to Christ. Our manner of life in Christ is a powerful part of our proclamation of the gospel.

Finally, some of the gifts of the Spirit are rooted in the choices we make. One of them is meekness, sometimes translated as self-control. Meekness is not self-depreciation; it is not running ourselves down. Rather, it is the quality of our focus. We are using the gifts God gave us in a focused, productive fashion. Space does not permit my dealing in depth with all of the fruits of the Spirit but they are a part of what we need to proclaim the gospel effectively. What and who we are is often our most powerful witness.

My oldest brother died last year after a long and lingering illness. The last years of his life were horrible. He was a veteran of World War II, he had many battle scars, and experienced extensive combat in the South Pacific in places like Okinawa and Iwo Jima. He was never the same after that. I suspect at times he envied his comrades who died in battle. Some days after he died, I came across some information from a *Second Lieutenant's Handbook*, a book printed for soldiers before they went into battle. One page in the handbook listed the essentials a soldier needed: ". . . take with you a bag, a canteen, a cup and meat can, knife, fork, spoon, wash basin, case helmet, tags, masks, gas masks, pistol, ammunition, a watch, a compass, field message book, first aid kit."[7]

A part of our "equipping" for the proclamation of the gospel is to be sure that we have the fruits of the Spirit going for us in our proclamation. Without them, we may never get a hearing for what it means to follow Jesus Christ. If Christ is real to us, our lives will showcase things like love, joy, peace, long-suffering, kindness, goodness, faithfulness, gentleness, and self-control. With those qualities shining through, all who meet us will have a picture of what being a follower of Jesus Christ is all about. Jesus is ready when you are.

For Reflection and Discussion

1. Can you share your most meaningful experience of the Holy Spirit?

2. When and where did God feel most real to you?

3. When you pray, do you stop speaking to listen for the voice of the Spirit?

4. List three experiences when you could feel the presence of God.

5. How have you seen the Holy Spirit at work in your church?
6. What evidence do you see of the fruits of the Spirit in your life? In your church?
7. How is the Holy Spirit helping your church to proclaim the gospel of Jesus Christ? What more could you do to work with the Spirit to proclaim the gospel?

11

Do People Really
Need Saving?

"I can put my trust and hope in Christ alone"
(Philippians 3:7—*The Living Bible*)

Sinners need a savior and Jesus Christ is the source of our salvation. The question of salvation is a real question. It is a question that needs to be settled in each of our lives.

Salvation marks the beginning point of our change of heart and our ways. Theologian Richard Niebuhr was confronted one day by a street evangelist who asked him bluntly if he was saved. Niebuhr reportedly said "I was saved by what Christ did; I am being saved right now; and I shall be saved when the Kingdom comes."[1]

Niebuhr is saying that salvation is the first step of an ongoing process. I believe that "once saved always saved." I also believe that as we live out our faith in Christ in this world, we should grow more and more in our likeness of Christ. The process of growing in our relationship to Christ is called "sanctification" and it continues throughout our lives.

The theme verse of this chapter grows out of the context of a problem in the early church. Paul, as we know, was commissioned to be a missionary to the Gentiles. He spent his life planting churches in Asia Minor, which was primarily Gentile. His was an urban strategy. He planted churches in the principle centers of commerce and culture. He did that until he was put in jail, and from his prison cell, he penned sixteen letters to those churches and to individuals to strengthen the churches. But there was a problem brewing. The population of Jerusalem, where the mother church was located, was primarily Jewish. Many of the early Christians were formerly Jewish. They would naturally reflect in their newfound faith in Christ some of their old ways. These people wanted the new Christians to be circumcised.

To Paul, and to others in the early church, requiring circumcision of non-Jewish Christians was unacceptable because it would send an ambivalent message about the Christian church. It is in this context that our theme verse is written: "We can put our trust and hope in Christ alone" (Philippians 3:7). Christ is sufficient for our salvation. It is upon Christ that we rely and place our hope.

The Need for Salvation

Why do we need salvation? We need salvation because we are sinners and "we are helpless to save ourselves" (Philippians 3:3). We need a savior to save us from our sins. A distinguished preacher once affirmed that two thoughts filled him with dread: the majesty of God and his own sense of sin. Any honest, candid assessment of who and what we are would cause any one of us to come to the same conclusion: we are sinners and we are in need of a savior.

We are born innocent, but we are not good. Moreover, we are born selfish. We enter this world with a strong desire to survive so we begin by wanting parents, food, or attention, and we leave a clear message with all those who love us that "If I do not get what I want when I want it, I will make life miserable for everybody."[2] It is perfectly normal for babies to behave that way; initially, it is the only way they know to get help. "I want it and I want it now" is the message they send out. But what works for a baby doesn't work for anyone else. We often hear the statements "I never met a bad kid" and "people are born basically good." I want to scuttle that illusion There *are* bad kids and bad people. None of us is born good. We can become good, but we are not born that way.[3] I still believe that there are more good people in the world than bad people but those who are good grow into it. The power of Christ can change us, redeem us, and make us new.

Aristides, when describing the early Christians to Emperor Hadrian, wrote "They love one another. They never fail to help widows; they save orphans from those who hurt them. If they have something they give freely to the person who has nothing; if they see a stranger, they take him home as a brother or sister in the spirit, the Spirit of God."[4] This moving description reaches across the centuries to remind us who and what we should be. But remember that the Christians were not born the way Aristides described them. They *became* what he described. They heard the proclamation of the gospel, responded to it, and were "made new in Christ."

I suspect that all of us can identify with that time and place when we knew unmistakably that we were not what God intended for us to be or what he wants us to be now. We are, in fact, sinners in need of salvation. Why else would David have cried out "Create in me a clean heart, O God" (Psalm 51:10 *NRSV*). It was because of the weight of his sin. Why did Isaiah the Prophet, who went up to the temple to pray, come down a new man? In the temple, in the presence of God, he took a new look at himself and cried out "I am a man of unclean lips" (Isaiah 6:5 *NRSV*). He not only looked at himself differently, but saw his peers and his contemporaries in a new light: "I dwell in the midst of a people with unclean lips . . ." (Isaiah 6:5 *NRSV*). A coal of fire from the altar touched his lips and he uttered a transforming sentence of commitment: "Here am I. Send me" (Isaiah 6:8 *NRSV*).

A sinner had been transformed. Isaiah had experienced the Grace of God in a life-changing way. Sooner or later (the sooner the better) we must come to God and acknowledge our sins.

One of the ways we proclaim the gospel of salvation is by making the sacraments of the church visible. At Peachtree Presbyterian, we have made baptism one of the most visible of our sacraments.

We baptize an average of thirty-nine adults each year. Our community of faith includes many of whom have not made a profession of faith before nor been baptized as infants. It is, therefore, a special moment of inspiration. The person to be baptized is called forward to the baptismal font. As they come forward, the congregation stands. The person then stands before me and the assembled congregation. The vows of church membership are given. The first vow is "Do you acknowledge that you are a sinner in the sight of God? A sinner in need of a Savior?" They answer "yes." The second vow is uttered: "Do you accept Christ as your Savior?" They answer "yes." These two vows, the heart of the matter, are followed by vows to do their best to "live as Christ would have them live," "to support his church in its worship and work," and to "live in Presbyterian ways." After the vows are affirmed by the person to be baptized, I ask him or her to kneel in the presence of the congregation and he or she is then baptized. I then say a prayer as the person begins the journey of faith. The person stands, I hold his or her hand and say:

> "Agreeable to the world of God in keeping with the standards of the Presbyterian Church in the United States of America, I declare that you are a member of Christ Church in the name of the Father, and of the Son, and of the Holy Spirit. Amen."

I then embrace the person who has been baptized and say "Go forth now and claim the full promise of your discipleship." The congregation welcomes them with joyous applause and the person returns to his or her seat surrounded by the community of faith, the church. An adult is never baptized in our church that other adults do not quickly step forward to begin their journey of faith in baptism.

Accepting the Promise

We all want what John Wesley wanted: "to know one thing—the way to heaven and how to land safely on that happy shore." We want, we need, we desire salvation. We want to make heaven our ultimate home but in reality, we resist salvation. We do this despite the fact that we are promised that "I can put my trust and hope in Christ alone."

How can anyone resist that promise and that hope? I think the issue is control. We have to surrender to accept the promise. We want to have our cake and eat it too. We surely want what Christ promises but we want to do it our way. We can change, but we resist that change.

I am told that among some African Christians, the New Testament word for redemption or salvation literally means "God took our heads out." It is an awkward phrase in English but reflects the history of much of Africa. In the Nineteenth Century, when slave trading was flourishing, white and black slave traders invaded villages and carried men, women, and children off to slavery. Each slave had an iron collar buckled around the neck which was attached to a chain. The chained were then taken to the coastline and shipped out to England or America. In this regard, the word redemption meaning "God took our heads out" makes moving sense. They were being set free in Christ to be all that God wanted them to be, that they were born to be. We can have all of that and more, but we have to give Christ control of our lives.[5]

We resist salvation because we want to retain control. The challenge is to surrender and live our lives in fellowship with Christ. Paul gives us the answer:

> "I have put aside all else . . . in order that I can have Christ and become one with him . . . trusting in Christ and Christ alone to save me" (Philippians 3:7. 8. 9—*The Living Bible*).

Our manner of living should be changed when we accept Christ as our Savior. We often fret over "our salvation" when we hear of the dramatic conversions of people we know. When we see the obvious change in their lives, we wonder about our own salvation which was not dramatic but instead gradual. I suspect this is more the norm; a gradual, growing awareness of a deepening response to Jesus Christ. One day we realized that we were his and he had become a friend, closer than a brother or sister. I have never known a day when Christ was not a part of my consciousness, but I can pinpoint moments in time when the presence of Christ was real in my experience. I treasure them as "holy moments" that were transforming. I was surrounded as a child by an environment where the gospel was proclaimed to me by godly parents, I was active in church, and learned the content of faith early. However, the way of our coming to salvation is not the important factor. The fact that we come to Christ is the important factor and our lives should reveal our relationship to him. More and more as we live, we should find ourselves walking in the footsteps of Christ.

Grace

Coming to know Jesus Christ should change the way we live. We are saved by grace, to be sure, but "by their fruits ye shall know them" (Matthew 7:20). W. H. Auden, after the Second World War, wrote two powerful lines which he called "Epitaph for the Unknown Soldier:"

"To save your world, you asked this man to die:
Would this man, could he see you now, ask why?"

What if Christ were to study the membership rolls of our churches and see how we are living, how we respond to the needs of others, and how we seek out the lonely and the lost? What would he think of us? When he sees us, does he ever wonder about dying for us? He would still die for us because of Grace. He knew who we were when he died for us: sinners in need of a Savior. The reality of our salvation challenges us to be "salt" and "light" in this world. The failure of our efforts is obvious. If we are "the salt of the earth" (Matthew 5:13), then why, in God's name and Christ's cause, is there so little flavor of what should be obvious in this world or in this nation? If we are to be "the light of the world" (Matthew 5:14), then why is there so much darkness about us and among us? Being saved does not mean that our redemptive mission is over but that it is just beginning.

Our world is under siege of hell and death, and where are we? It must concern us all when:

three children are raped and sexually mutilated by three teenagers in a Satanic ritual;

the most expensive item in an antique mall in Buckhannon, West Virginia, is a KKK paperweight;

a 1992 USA Today investigation of the nation's racially motivated murders during the Twentieth Century revealed that in the overwhelming majority of cases, no one was ever brought to justice;

twelve million children go hungry every day in the United States;

our country lurches, at the highest levels, from one scandal to another; and

mainline denominations are reporting their thirtieth straight year of membership loss[6]

If anyone doubts that the gospel needs renewed proclamation for the salvation of humankind, look around you every day. If anyone doubts that the church needs to experience renewal, look around you on Sunday. Salvation is both an event and a process. We come to a moment of certainty, then we live each day striving to make our lives worthy of the one we call Savior and Lord.

One of the most helpful stories from the Desert Fathers has been retold by Kathleen Norris in *Dakota: A Spiritual Geography*. Abbot Lot went to see Abbot Joseph and said "Father, according as I am able, I keep my little rule and my little fast, my prayer, meditation, and contemplative silence; and according as I am able, I strive to cleanse my heart of bad thoughts. Now what more should I do?" The elder Abbot stretched out his hands to heaven. His hands became like lamps of fire and he said "Why not become all flame?"[7]

I pray that I will live to see our church a flaming fire for God. Then we would be "the salt of the earth" and "the light of the world."

For Reflection and Discussion

1. Some say that there is a crisis of belief in the American church and that we really do not believe that Christ is essential for salvation. What do you think?

2. When you look into the mirror, do you see yourself as a person who needs to change your ways?

3. Do we really take seriously the fact that when we make a profession of faith in Christ that we begin by acknowledging that we are sinners?

4. The sacraments are outward signs of an inward working of the spirit. How visible are they in your church?

5. When was the last time an adult was baptized in your church in the presence of the congregation?

6. How concerned are you in your congregation about the salvation of men and women in your community? Most believe that one-half of the American population is unchurched. Have you conducted a survey to get the facts on your community? Have you considered the possibility that there may be a mission field at your door?

7. Do you know any adults in your circle of friends who has never made a profession of faith? Have you ever shared with them what your faith means to you?

8. When did you finally know the love of Christ? How have you experienced God's grace in your life? Did you share your story with others?

9. How is God's saving grace still at work in your life?

10. How is your church proclaiming the gospel so others might know of God's saving grace?

12

Me an Evangelist?
You've Got to be Kidding!

"The harvest truly is great, but the laborers are
few . . ." (Luke 10:2—*New King James Version*)

I sometimes think that people either have too much religion or not enough. Some "evangelists" offend us.
Their words feel more like an assault than loving concern about where we are in our relationship to Jesus
Christ. Then there are people who feel that religion is so
private we should not intrude upon that subject with
anyone. We should not share beliefs. We Presbyterians,
in some circles, almost cringe when we hear the word
"evangelism."

An "evangel" is one who has a story to tell or an announcement to make. An evangelist is one who goes
out to tell the story of Jesus Christ: how he lived, how
he died, how he rose again from the dead. If there is no
Resurrection, there is no story to tell. So to be an evangelist, you have to believe something before you can be
something.

In the church, we have more or less concluded that
evangelism is the work of the professionals, primarily
the clergy. They are the "experts" and only "experts"
should be involved in evangelism. How can we recon-
cile this with the church's history? For its first three hundred years, the church did not have ordained clergy. It
conquered the Roman Empire for Christ because the
"believers" understood that they had been sent on a
mission by the living Christ. The Presbyterian Church
(USA) now has fewer members than the United Presby-

terian Church had in 1965. When we lament the massive decline (38 percent) in the membership of our denomination (1,627,295 members since 1965), we raise the indignant question "Why doesn't the church do something about this situation?" What we mean by "church" is, why doesn't the *clergy* do something about this decline?

We *can* do something about this situation, but it must involve us all. The members of the church, all of us, must become evangelists and tell the story. We must turn our churches into armies of believers and go out and tell the story. What an opportunity we have with half of the American population unchurched! Churches that are growing today have the membership mobilized in telling the story of Jesus Christ. The effort is intentional. The Christian church from the beginning did not experience "automatic growth." It was the product of intention and hard work. A church in Atlanta has a sign in its parking lot that reads "You are now entering the mission field." This church is right on target. My friend Bruce Larson reminds me that "Jesus did not tell the world to go to church. He told the church to go to the world."

We must overcome our reluctance to evangelize. The telling of the story, which is the most natural way, involves the people of God in the proclamation of the gospel. At the foundation of our evangelism is what we believe about Jesus Christ personally. If we do not believe that Christ can and does make a difference in a person's life, then we do not have a story to tell. Our "dilemma" about evangelism may, in fact, reveal a crisis of belief in the church and its members. But assuming that we do believe, and we are willing to tell the story, what should we expect when we share our faith with another?

First, it will not be easy. It is not easy because every person that you meet is different. This conversation between a college professor and a minister will give you a flavor of things to come. The professor and the minister were close friends. The professor observed to his friend that he could not understand why he should invite people to come to church: "I cannot figure out what makes the church different from other organizations. Our peacher is always urging us to invite someone to church with us. He says that we need new members. And as I sit there while the preacher talks, I ask myself 'Why would I invite anyone to be a part of this?'"

He was not against the church and what was happening on Sunday morning, mind you. "It's just . . ." "Just what?" asked his friend. The professor continued: "Well, he said, the reality is I don't see anything different about what is happening at church than what I am experiencing in any number of locations and organizations. If you talk about friendliness and caring and community service, you can get that in a good Rotary Club. The preacher when he preaches is just giving good advice, but the same kind of advice can be had in any number of places. As a matter of fact, Rotary meets at a more convenient time of the week than church."[1]

It would be a challenge to respond to that wouldn't it? It strikes to the heart of our unique mission. What is it that sets us apart from a civic club? The evangelist should be able to articulate his or her faith and its uniqueness. There is no substitute for vital church involvement.

The professor, however, raises a valid question that the church and its people must be equipped to answer.

Recently, in the journal *First Things*, three scholars reported the results of efforts to discern why mainline American Protestantism (Methodists, Lutherans, Episcopalians, Presbyterians, and United Church of Christ) has experienced massive declines in membership. They concluded that "The best single predicator of church participation turned out to be belief, orthodox Christian belief, especially the teaching that a person can be saved through Jesus Christ."[2]

What sets the church apart from any civic club is what it believes about Jesus Christ. Our belief defines who we are. The church is the only organization on earth that requires us to admit publicly that we are sinners before we join. Believing in Jesus Christ is the central conviction that has driven the church through the centuries, and it is the absence of this central conviction that has eroded our membership. Researchers say that it has depleted the ranks of the Presbyterian Church in particular. The data indicates that 68 percent of the lay members of the Presbyterian Church do not believe that there is "no other name under heaven . . . whereby we are saved."[3]

Common Obstacles and Excuses

We are sent out to tell the story of Jesus Christ. Without belief we have no story to tell. The church advances when its members, out of the foundation of their personal faith, share with others and reach out to them. I find it refreshing that many of the persons I encounter who are seeking or exploring the meaning of faith are honest and open to truth and dialogue. However, I also have encountered a variety of excuses. A helpful little volume by Michael Green entitled *You Must Be Joking: Popular Excuses for Avoiding Jesus Christ*, has been a blessing to me. I recommend it to pastors and evangelism committees throughout our churches. It is practical and it is connected with what is real. According to Green, the most poplar excuses are discussed below in more detail.

"I'm not the Religious Sort"

This is nonsense; we are all religious. God made us religious. We will worship something; it is just a question of what. This is an excuse pure and simple. It may, in fact, be a reaction to some of the things the church is doing. For example, long, boring services, with little or no connection to life, seem out of touch to some people who conclude that the "religious sorts" are out of touch. The church is not perfect, however, and it is made up of persons who have publicly acknowledged their sinfulness. The church has been a mixed bag of folk since the beginning. Of the Disciples, all hand-picked by Jesus of Nazareth, one betrayed him, one denied him, some had excessive ambitions for power, and all but one, John the beloved Disciple, fled the city after Jesus' arrest, trial, scourging, and Crucifixion.

But basic to who we are is the desire for a transcendent connection. We are all religious. And Christianity is about relationships. First, there is the restoration of our relationship to God, then the restoration of our relationship with others. Those who have experienced such restoration will reach out to others to share their new-found relatedness to the One who "loves us and gave himself for us." "I'm not the religious sort" can be a conversation stopper or expressed with a longing wistfulness as in "I wish I had a faith like yours but I don't."[4]

"You Can't Believe in God These Days"

These are times that bewilder and are out of joint. But interestingly enough, in spite of it, opinion polls show that overwhelming majorities in Western countries do believe in God. One cannot so easily dismiss the maker of heaven and earth with a trite disclaimer that "you can't believe in God these days." I have always liked the statement attributed to Dr. Jowett, head of Oxford College: "It is not what I think of God, but what God thinks of me."[5]

There are may barriers to a belief in God. There is the irrationality of human suffering. We often cannot fathom, and the heart refuses to accept, the injustice of suffering by those we love and cherish. But God is not immune to pain. He does not take callous delight in our suffering. He promises us that he is with us always. Jesus Christ, his only Son, our Lord, walked the dusty roads of Galilee. He knew thirst and hunger, friendship and rejection, fear and isolation, and his life ended in one of the most inhumane ways a person can die.[6]

Some find belief in God a challenge because life seems so meaningless, and this theme is captured in much of today's music.

Yet when you add up all of the excuses for not believing in God, you also have to take into account the reality of religion. We are incurably religious. The Soviet Union tried to banish God but failed. The Chinese tried the same in China but they failed. When you share your story, listen carefully to all of the excuses. They are real to the persons making them but it does not matter because there is an inner urging within them and in us that is reaching for God.

"All Religions Lead to God"

We tell our story in all of its uniqueness, not because we disrespect the stories of other faiths but because Jesus Christ gave it to us, entrusted to us the telling of his story.

The statement "all religions lead to God" is not a new idea. Paul, when he arrived in ancient Athens, viewed the plethora of religious monuments, observed that they seemed to thrive on many gods. Be that as it may, he wanted to talk to them of the unknown God. These Athenians were touching all of the basics for they had a monument to "The Unknown God." Paul built on this local reality and began to speak to them about Jesus Christ.

We respect the religions of others who come from other cultures. We are experiencing increasing religious diversity in this country. Michael Green asserts that it is "illogical" to assume that all religions are pointing in the same direction. For example, the goal of all existence in Buddhism is "nirvana," extinction attained by Buddha after 547 births. The goal of all existence in Christianity is to know God and enjoy him forever.[7]

The mercy of God is "from everlasting to everlasting." In Jesus Christ it is revealed as the hymn writer phrased it: "A wideness in God's mercy like the wideness of the Sea . . ."

I believe as others do that Jesus Christ is the light of the world and in him there is no darkness. The New Testament makes it very clear who are lost. It is not those who have never heard; it is those who have heard and said "no."[8]

"Jesus was Just a Good Man"

A young man came to see me several years ago. He acknowledged that he was very drawn to Christianity and to Jesus Christ as a role model. He simply could not "buy" that he was and is the Son of God, our Savior. As far as I know, he has never been able to accept Jesus

Christ. Even those who cannot *accept* Jesus' uniqueness acknowledge it. His character was like no other. His claims were different and his teaching set him apart. His behavior was different. He taught that we should live by high standards and he kept them. His capacities were different. He caused the lame to walk, the blind to see, the weak to become strong, those with confused minds to recover reason, and his words had the ring of truth and authority.

It comes down to a choice; a decisive choice, a life altering choice. Is Jesus who he claimed to be or not? If he is, then he can be your Savior and mine. If he is not, then as you say, "Jesus was just another good man."

"It Doesn't Matter What You Believe as Long as You are Sincere"

It matters incredibly what we believe. Hitler was sincere about what he believed but it was madness. His madness plunged the world into darkness and war. The cult victims in California were sincere but misdirected, and their cultic suicide shocked our nation. The Pharisees were sincere but they conceived the "law of God" which defined right living an intolerable burden on the people. They had become so preoccupied with the letter of the law they lost sight of its purpose which is to liberate and set us free. One author has called the law of God "liberating limits." Again and again, we are called upon to believe. Belief requires a definite commitment to Christ.

"I do My Best; No One can do More"

What happens when you do not do your best? It is not going to be good enough. We all want to rationalize our way into God's good graces. We say "I know that I am not perfect, but I'm trying to do my best. I'm doing the best that I can with the Ten Commandments and I am sure that God knows that I am." A commitment to Christ places us in relationship with Christ. That relationship is lived out in the church where we are nourished and reinforced by other believers. To hide behind the excuse of doing our best is to avoid the central question of commitment.

"Nothing can Alter My Past"

This conjures up pictures of a misspent life too bad to mention or too far gone for help. In the previous excuse, we were dealing with a person whose past was not perfect, but who believed that "doing his or her best" would somehow atone for it. Here, we are dealing with a person who believes that nothing can be done. There is no grace that will be sufficient for this person's needs.[9]

"When You're Dead, You're Dead"

"When I die, I rot" said Bertrand Russell. No one can argue with the factual accuracy of that statement but that is not the whole story. Jesus said "because I live you shall live also" (John 14:19). He affirmed "I am the Resurrection and the life . . ."

A young man and his wife visited our church and had come to discuss membership with me. I asked him "What's holding you back?" He held up his hand and moved his thumb and forefinger so close to touching that you could barely see the space that existed between them, and said "I am this close." I asked him what theological barrier was represented by the minuscule distance. He answered with two words: "The Resurrection."

He was not only not close, he was not even in the neighborhood. No Resurrection, no hope; no New Testament, no church; and to quote Paul, we of "all people would be the most miserable." I told him "John, you are not close at all. There is more, much more, to making a commitment to Jesus Christ. The Resurrection is the heart of it all."

Some weeks later, I received him into the church on profession of faith and baptism. This fall, he will be ordained as a minister. Jesus was very dead but now he is very alive. This central reality is the source of our hope.

"You Can't Change Human Nature"

If I believed that, I could no longer preach. I am confident that all of us have certain preconditions, both from our environment and from our genes, but we can change. Paul affirmed that in Christ " . . . all things have become new" (II Corinthians 5:17). "All things" include you and me. I have seen enemies forgive, habits abandoned, marriages mended, and lifestyles and attitudes altered, all because of a relationship with Jesus Christ.[10]

As you begin to tell your story of your journey with Jesus Christ, you are going to hear all kinds of excuses. Be sure to give evidence of your care for the person to whom you are speaking. This was brought home to me on a recent airplane trip. I was in my seat when a man sat down beside me. He did not speak when I spoke to him and he seemed preoccupied. Then I saw him put a Bible into his lap. He cleared his throat and asked me "Are you saved?" I said "Yes, I am."

He did not seem to hear me and proceeded to explain to me in some detail the plan of salvation, thumbing through his Bible to find proof texts of his assertions. I sat there in amazement. Here was a man of zeal who, as far as I knew, was an earnest believer. But he had not even introduced himself to me. I did not know his name and he did not know mine. The longer he talked, the more I felt like a victim of his zeal. I could see him adding my name to those who had been "saved" by his witness to me on an airplane as we made our way across the country. But I was somewhat relieved that he could not add my name because he did not know it.

He finally concluded his explanation of the plan of salvation and asked me the essential question of "Do you accept Christ as your personal Savior?"

I responded that I had accepted Jesus Christ more than fifty years ago. Before he could catch his breath, I told him that I had been reared in a Christian home, nurtured by Christian parents, and could never consciously remember a day when I did not believe in Jesus Christ. I then told him my name, my profession, and that I had been the pastor of the church that I was then servicing for more than twenty-five years. He moved to another seat on the airplane.

I meant no offense. In fact, I admired his zeal but thought that he would have been far more effective if he had gotten to know the person to whom he was speaking. When we tell our story of how Christ has made a difference in our lives, we should begin by getting to know the person. Let them tell us their story. Learn about their family and religious experience. Then in a natural way, tell your story of what Christ has meant in your life.

The Responsibility is Ours

We are living in an unchurched society. The reality of that is a challenge but also an opportunity. We are surrounded by many people who are seeking because they sense that something is missing in their lives. Each person is different so expression of their needs is different. Some say "I think what is missing is spiritual; I need something spiritual in my life." Others say "There must be something more for me. I want to feel like my life is making a difference, counting for something." There are seekers working in the office where you work, in the law office where you practice law, on the street where you live, and in the school where you teach. Be sensitive to them and prepared to tell them your story.

Jesus sent his Disciples out two by two after he had been barred from his hometown synagogue by his own people. It was the second time that it had happened. It happened because they did not believe, would not accept the claims that were being made about him. They had doubtless heard the stories of the lame walking, the blind regaining their sight, and how people were being changed and helped. They simply would not believe the stories were true. He was just another village boy and they had watched him grow for thirty-three years. The rejection was real and painful. It always is when it comes from those we know and love. The rejection was not inconsequential because in Mark, we are told that no mighty work could be done there (Mark 6:5).

Our family likes to go to the beach. We also like our grandchildren to be with us. We have wonderful family days together. Early in the morning when the sun is making its way across the sky, the children get up and before long are saying "Let's go to the beach!" Have you noticed that when you go down to the beach with your grandchildren, you carry a lot of stuff? I have also noticed that whatever you take to the beach multiples once you get it there. One morning, I was loaded with "beach stuff." I looked and my youngest grandson, just three years old, who was just strolling along. He was not carrying a thing! As a matter of fact, when he noticed that I was looking at him, he suggested that it might be good if I carried him! I noticed the little shirt he was wearing with the inscription "Share God's Gifts—Serve One Another". That was the theme of our Bible School. When we proclaim the gospel, that is what we do. When we tell another about what God has done for us, how God has been there for us, we are sharing his gifts and serving one another. That is how the word got around about Jesus Christ from the very beginning. They went from village to village, traveling light, staying in homes and telling the story. They were not to focus on rejection and failure but were to "shake the dust off their feet and go on to the next village." Today, we do not have to travel anywhere; the seekers may be next door or in the next office.

Why is it we hesitate? We talk about everything else when we get together with people: the current sports news, what's happening in town, and who's coming to town. We share everything but what we have experienced with Christ in our lives. It is almost an unwritten conspiracy that we are not to talk about Jesus Christ. We often conclude that our story is so "private" or religion is so "private" that it is unmentionable. So we lose natural opportunities to share our faith.

There is a great need in the world around us for us to share our story. Joseph Campbell said that the majority of his friends were living a "wasteland life." There are people that we rub shoulders with routinely who are just holding on with quiet desperation. Many people are there. They need to hear your story and mine.

We should be active about telling the story. Jesus did not say "Think about this, meditate on this, and see what you think." He said get up and get going! Jim Wallace was interviewed in Watts in Los Angeles after the riots that destroyed property and hope for many. He was trying in a particular way to deal with some of the gangs in the area. He met one day with a group of gang leaders and said to them "The Church of Jesus Christ is interested in coming out here to help you. What can we do?" He was startled when one of the most influential gang leaders in Watts said "You might consider leading us to the Lord."

We need to be telling the story and taking initiatives to reach out to the seekers. The story is transforming. Tell your story with joy and with expectation, the expectation that God will use it for good. Quit fretting. God expects all of us to be evangelists. If your story is authentic, it will have a power of its own that God can and will use. We need to be telling our story if we have one. If we don't, Christ is waiting to help us share the story of his presence in our lives.

For Reflection and Discussion

1. Did you ever consider that you are an evangelist?

2. How active is your church in follow-up with a visitor to your church?

3. Do you have a negative evangelism committee in your church?

4. Do you in your church really care whether you grow or not?

5. In the last five years, did your church have an increase or a decrease in membership?

6. List ten recent excuses you have heard for spasmodic participation in the church. Can you think of some that you have made in the last six months?

7. Do you feel that "salvation by works" is a concept that dies hard in each of our faith journeys?

8. Do you believe that sharing your story of Christ is easier if you know the person's story to whom you are speaking?

9. Do you feel intimidated at your work at the point of your witness for Christ?

10. Are you aware of the faith of the coworkers at your place of employment?

11. If you know of unchurched neighbors or friends have you invited them to church?

12. Do you honestly believe that Christ makes a difference in a person's life?

13. Do you believe that Christ can and does make a difference in your life? How? Have you told others about this belief?

14. How would you respond to the excuses given in this chapter?

15. In small groups, tell each other what Christ has meant in our lives. Listen to others as they share their stories.

13

When all is Said and Done, What will be Said and Done?

". . . and the Lord added to the church daily those who were being saved" (Acts 2:47—*The New King James Version*)

My concern in this book has been to impede what I discern as a deadly drift in the Presbyterian Church USA (PCUSA), as well as all mainline denominations. There is but one way to drift and that is down. We cannot aimlessly confront the Twenty-first Century with our fingers crossed, hoping and praying that this will somehow or another work out. We have both the capacity and the resources to be more than we are, all that God would have us be. We have a mission to claim and tremendous opportunities to seize but time is moving swiftly.

We must face the reality that ours is a church in massive decline as the erosion of our membership continues. We are a church divided and the season of acrimony continues. Many feel there is no common ground that unites us anymore and some believe that we are struggling for the very soul of the Presbyterian witness in this nation. I believe that the six Great Ends of the Church can be a rallying point, a place of common ground, if we will cast aside our militant, and sometimes petty, agendas to grasp the framework that can define our witness.

"The proclamation of the gospel for the salvation of humankind" is the heart of the church's witness. If we do not rally around this central mission, then we can accept no others and there is no hope for the other Great Ends of the Church.

We have danced around the issue of the loss of membership for years in the Presbyterian Church. We have said "All that we do is evangelism." It is easy to take that statement and make the central task of the church, which is the proclamation of the gospel, a general concern, not the primary concern. The "business" of the church is to reach the unreached, the lost. In their recent book, *What Unites Presbyterians*, the Stated Clerk of our Assembly, Clifton Kirkpatrick and William H. Hopper, Jr., said the reasons for our decline are threefold:[1]

1. New church development has slowed. This is certainly true. I am encouraged that there seems to be a renewed interest in new church development in all regions of the church.

2. Presbyterians have not been able to retain the children and youth born to Presbyterian families. The actual statement is "Presbyterians have not produced sufficient offspring." That we are not able to "retain" the children is a serious indictment on the quality of our work and witness and perhaps our family life.

3. The United States is increasingly a racial and ethnic nation but the Presbyterian Church (USA) is predominantly white Anglo-Saxon. This is reality and we will not be increasingly racial ethnic until we are willing to adjust our polity to accommodate other forms of worship. I have never, in my entire ministry, served a church that was unwilling to receive racial ethnic persons and the church that I now serve has a higher percentage of racial ethnics than the Presbyterian Church (USA).

I have no dispute with Kirkpatrick and Hopper's three reasons, but the reality of our decline is more basic. I believe that Kirkpatrick and Hopper are right on target when they say "The sometimes unstated fact is that the Presbyterian Church has not changed its historic pattern of not being very vocal about telling others about Christ."[2]

Unless we change this reality, we will continue to decline and to be divided. A declining church becomes, at least in its structures, preoccupied with survival. There is a tendency to become regulatory. Regulations, in a community that is a volunteer association, cause reactions. The reactions siphon off energy and resources that could be used for the proclamation of the gospel for the salvation of humankind. When a church becomes more concerned about its structures than its redemptive purpose, it is going to decline. And it should.

Facing the Issues

I believe that our decline can be reversed and our church renewed. We can yet claim our promise under God, but time is of the essence and we must find the common cause to act now. It is not going to be easy. There are five issues that we must face.

1.   We must choose.

We have to decide, choose what we believe about Jesus Christ. Do we believe that to decide for him makes a difference in the lives of individuals and in the life of the church? If we do, we must proclaim it and live it. A large part of our dilemma is a crisis of belief, both in our clergy and in our members. The church, our church, has sent many uncertain messages about what we really believe about Jesus Christ.

I know that we have our creeds, our Book of Order, and we say a lot of things that are foundational, but right down where we live and serve, our witness is often not as clear as our standards. William Lippmann, in *A Preface to Morals*, noted that liberal churchmen have been highly ambivalent about what they believe. Lippmann said what was missing was "that ineffable certainty which once made God and His Plan seem as real as the lamp-post."[3] I think William Willimon, Dean of the University Chapel at Duke, is absolutely right in his portrayal of a "Christ centered church" as ". . . a political and ideological monkey wrench thrown into the culture."[4]

The culture that surrounds us is much into "What's in it for me?" We are preoccupied with ourselves. We want a "designer religion," one of our own making, but there is more and more evidence that this religion does not fulfill the spiritual void that is at the center of our hearts. So we are surrounded by seekers, people who are earnestly looking for something more. In large measure, the church that is clear about what it believes about Jesus Christ is a church that is growing and making a difference in its community.

Research indicates that Jesus is more important in the minds of many of our seekers than is the church. A friend, a regular visitor to our church, stated to me "I love Jesus, but I don't like the church." Many people feel the same way. The church is seen as an institution when it needs to be regarded as a movement that is centered on its choice that Jesus Christ makes a difference.

Patrick Morley, in his book *The Seven Seasons of a Man's Life*, tells the story of two Americans who came into a shop one day is Israel. It was a shop run by a remarkable Arab-Christian named Ferridah who is called "The Mother Teresa of Israel." Out of her little shop she has supported six hundred orphans and started two orphanages and a children's hospital. She takes in abandoned Muslim widows without families and teaches them how to sew for a living. The two Americans in the shop began to argue. Knowing that Ferridah was an Arab, they began to make disparaging remarks about Arabs, especially about those who lived in that quarter of the old city of Jerusalem. A third American who stood in the shop chastised the two men for their insensitive and unkind remarks. Ferridah simply observed "You Americans are so interesting. You take your Bible literally, but you don't take it seriously."[5]

If we are to renew our church in the Twenty-first Century, we have to take seriously what we believe, about the Bible and about Jesus Christ.

2.   We must face the challenge of renewal

The promise before us is great, but the challenge is also great. How do you reverse he trend of the decline?

There are some fine books that address this very question. One of the best is John Killinger's book entitled *Preaching to a Church in Crisis: A Homiletic for the Last Days of the Mainline Church*. It is difficult to conceive, but the Episcopalians, Methodists, Disciples of Christ, Lutherans, American Baptists, and Presbyterians (USA), during a fifteen-year period, sustained losses of 5,000 members a week. This is closing the equivalent of one 700-member church a day every day for fifteen years. The loss of members is not the full story, however. Mainline denominations during the same period of time lost 15 percent of their preference in the polls.[6]

Where is the opportunity for renewal? The opportunity is in the thousands of people who are seeking some sense of spiritual security and peace. For, as George Gallup, Jr., and Jim Castelli reported, "The baseline of religious belief is remarkably high, certainly, the highest of any developed nation in the world."[7]

The climate in which we minister is one of contradiction. On the one hand, there are those who think the church is unnecessary to their lives. Some people conclude that they can be spiritual without it. In the movie "The Color Purple," Alice Walker has one of her characters demand:

> "Tell the truth, have you ever found God in Church? I never did. I just found a bunch of folks hoping for him to show. Any god I ever felt in church I brought in with me."[8]

On the other hand, there are many like the person Douglas Copeland described in his book *Life After God* that voices the longing that many of us feel as we face life today without the spiritual resources to see us through:

> "I think I am a broken person. I seriously question the road that I have taken and I endlessly rehash the compromises I have made in my life. I have an insecure . . . job with an amoral corporation so I don't

have to worry about money. I put up with halfway relationships so as not to have to worry about loneliness. I have lost the ability to recapture the purer feelings of my younger years in exchange for a streamlined narrow-mindedness that I assumed would propel me to 'the Top.' What a joke!"[7]

The person continues:

"Now here is my secret . . . I need God! I need God to help me to give . . . to help me to be kind . . . to help me to love . . ."[9]

Here is our opportunity. I have heard that story as a minister hundreds of times. The faces are different, the names are different, but the inner longing is the same. The warm-hearted, caring, welcoming community of faith will reap an abundant harvest for Jesus Christ in the Twenty-first Century if we have the courage to be the church. People want something about God that is real, that connects with their lives. Our people live in a constant tension with what their heart yearns for and what their culture offers them.

The opportunity is unlimited for the proclamation of the gospel.

3.   Changes
It can no longer be business as usual in the church. Most mainline American Protestant churches are operating on a '50s model, a model that did well in what was basically a churched society. The scene is vastly different today as we are living, serving, and proclaiming the gospel in an unchurched society. People are dealing with the proliferation of knowledge. Over 400,000 books are published in the United States annually, over a thousand new books a day in our country alone.[11] The world has become smaller because of our capacity to communicate by fax, telephone, and e-mail, and to travel great dis-

tances in a short time. Massive changes are underway in medicine, genetic engineering, and laser surgery.

The church, while it has a story that was "once delivered to the saints," must take advantage of this change and use it for redemptive purposes. For example, e-mail can be an effective means of contacting people to proclaim the gospel.

While changes bring disruption and uncertainty, the other side of cultural disruption and uncertainty is opportunity for the church in the proclamation of the gospel. People need inner resources to cope with change.

The church in its witness and proclamation can point the way. The changes that face us represent the greatest opportunity for the church in my lifetime and perhaps for any time. Leonard Sweet, dean at Drew University Theological School, identified "24 Transitions for the 21st Century." I will pick a few of them to stimulate your thinking about the future of your church in your town or community. He suggests that for the church to claim its promise in the new century, it must change from:

its practice of critique and pick-apart to celebrate and pick up;

critical thinking to creative thinking;

representation to participation;

institutional "Here I Stand" churchianity (maintenance) to "There We Go" Christianity (mission);

inwardly mobile to outwardly mobile ministry: turn on the headlights, not the dome lights.

authority structures to relational structures.

asking "does it make sense" to "was it a good experience?"

integrity to authenticity;

theology of giving to theology of receiving;

church growth to church health; and

Christendom Culture (church-broken) to Pre-Christian Mission Fields (the unchurched and the over-churched)[12]

We should not fear change in the church but embrace it. Have we forgotten the ringing affirmation of Paul: "if anyone is in Christ they are a new creation, the old has passed away, the new has come" (II Corinthians 5:17).

4.   Commitment.
If we are to claim our promise and be true to our heritage as Christians and as Presbyterians, we must make some basic commitments and promises. The proclamation of the gospel begins with our own personal commitment to Christ. The late Dr. George W. Truett is a near legendary figure in Southern Baptist circles. One of the stories told about him tells of a challenge concerning Christian stewardship that he was making.

Dr. Truett was urging his listeners to give of their financial resources to God. He made it clear that Christian stewardship is rooted in one's personal acceptance of Jesus Christ. As this scene unfolds ". . . the Deacons passed around very large wicker baskets. In the back of the sanctuary a little boy off the streets, an urchin who had nothing to give, asked for the deacons to put the basket on the floor. The little boy got into the basket. He said, 'I'll give me.'"[13]

If we are to renew our church and proclaim the gospel, we must begin with you saying—and my saying—"I'll give me."

There are those who believe that we are already in the beginning stages of a new great awakening in America. Many church people have expressed their concern about the health of the church in America but they are also expressing hope. John Killinger says if we are to claim the promise of the Twenty-first Century for

Christ, the church must be seen as a movement again and not as an institution. George Hunter, III, professor of mission and evangelism at Asbury Theological Seminary in Wilmore, Kentucky, says that we must become an Apostolic Church and argues for a return to the basics. Hunter identifies the eleven distinctive features of the Apostolic Church which I believe can be a valuable guide.

1. Apostolic congregations seek to root believers and seekers in Scripture for after all, the Bible is the content of the faith.

2. Apostolic congregations are disciplined in their prayer life.

3. Members believe great things about God and expect great things from God. Everyone in the church has a prayer partner and there is an overt emphasis on prayer throughout the life of the congregation.

4. Apostolic congregations have a passion and compassion for lost, unchurched people. The underlying passion in every church should be that "lost people matter to God."

5. Apostolic congregations obey the great commission. They accept it as a privilege, not as a duty to be performed. The main business of the church is to make faith possible for the unreached. Outreach is not one of many ministries of the church; it *is* the ministry of the church.

6. Apostolic congregations have a vision for what men and women disciples can become.

7. Apostolic congregations are relevant, adapting to the language, music, and style of the people they are trying to reach.

8. Apostolic congregations seek to involve everyone—members and seekers—in a small group where they can be nourished spiritually.

9. Apostolic congregations seek the involvement of all laity in ministries where they are gifted. They seek to discern the gifts of the people and let them express those gifts through involvement in the church ministry.

10. Apostolic congregations care about pastoral care and seek persons who are gifted in shepherding care.

11. Apostolic congregations have many ministries that focus on the unchurched who have not found Christ.[14]

In the movie "Sister Act," Whoopi Goldberg is a nightclub performer in Las Vegas who witnesses a murder. To protect her, the police hide her in a Roman Catholic convent. She adopts the habit of a nun and goes to worship with them. The church is lacking in spirit and joy and the choir is a drag.

She accepts the challenge of doing something about the choir and the place comes alive. People on the street hear the music and begin to come inside the church. There is obviously a reaction, and the Mother Superior decides that Whoopi cannot lead the choir anymore. A priest, meanwhile, speaks to the Reverend Mother, telling her how much he has enjoyed the Mass, the music, and the obvious joy in the church and ends his affirmation by saying ". . . Did you see the people walk right in from the street? That music, that heavenly music! Reverend Mother, it called to them."

She replied: "It . . . it did?"[15]

We must in our commitment to Christ be open to the spirit of God leading us out to places where we have never been before. I believe that when we get "out" to those places we will find our Lord there. He is always going before us. He is out there waiting for the Presbyterian Church (USA) to come out to where he is, where the people are who are seeking him and reaching for his help and strength.

This spring, I was in London to speak at a preaching conference. I noted a revival of the play "Jesus Christ

Superstar" and went to see it. The stage performance was one of the most moving experiences of my life. The Crucifixion scene of Jesus of Nazareth was graphic and gripping. The play ended with them taking the lifeless body of Jesus down from the cross, and with armed guards surrounding the body, they made their way toward the tomb. The ghastly deed had been done. The curtain came down and there was silence. In the silence there was weeping, and then there was thunderous applause. I can still see in my mind's eye the scenes of that play. I can still see myself in the character that portrayed Judas for there is something of the betrayer in us all.

The curtain lifted and the cast began to present themselves. Applause greeted each of them. Then the actor who portrayed Judas ran from the wings to center stage. He had done a magnificent job; but there was little applause and the little there was was muted. It seemed so inappropriate to applaud a betrayer. As the play ended and they carried the body of Jesus of Nazareth away, I thought "All of this he has done for me. What have I every really done for him?"

If we love him and believe in him, we will tell the story. The absence of proclamation means the absence of faith.

I have undertaken the challenge of writing this book for the church, not because I am a great writer or because I have anything unique to say. I have done it because I have a passion, a deep passion to tell the story of Jesus and his love. In writing this book I have prayed that our Lord, by his spirit, would use it to make alive our cold hearts, still hands, and quiet voices so that we would be fired with a new awareness of Jesus Christ and that together, we can begin new initiatives in his name. I long to see the real capacities of this church of ours unleashed for Jesus Christ.

In England, my wife and I worshipped at evensong in Coventry Cathedral. It is a striking cathedral, blending the ruins of the old with the new. It is a cathedral that literally rose out of the rubble of war to become a special place of worship and service. Bombs rained down on the old cathedral from the sky during World War II. After the war, young people from Germany came over to help clean up the rubble and ruin. The architect who was commissioned to build the new cathedral left the ruins of the old, the tower, as a kind of forecourt before entering into the new section.

In a niche on a side aisle, there is a head of Christ. It was done by an Arizona artist and the head is made from the metal taken from the wreckage of automobiles. The whole Christian religion is represented in that head. An artist takes pieces from car wrecks and makes the head of Christ. God takes the wreckage of what I am and what you are and makes us new. He draws us together in his church and calls us "the body of Christ." He then sends us into the world to tell the story of his love. Have you told the story lately? Do you have a story to tell about how he has changed you?

For Reflection and Discussion

1. What action steps would you take to renew and revitalize the church?

2. Do you believe it is the nature and mission of the church to grow?

3. What are you willing to do to renew the church where you are a member?

14

Membership Does Matter

"Each day God added to them all who were being saved" Acts 2:47—*Living Bible*)

S ome years ago there came from our General Assembly a popular phrase: "Theology Matters." Theology does matter. We have to believe something before we can be something. The final proof of a vital theology is a vital, courageous, responding church.

I became the pastor of the Peachtree Presbyterian Church in Atlanta, Georgia, twenty-six years ago. On my arrival in the city, I visited many of the ministers who had been serving in our city for some time. One visit was unforgettable, as was the minister. I asked him what he thought of the prospects of having a growing church on the north side of Atlanta. He replied that he had no idea whether there was an opportunity for growth or not. He then asserted that perhaps he was not the person to be asked that question and said "I have a philosophy that if someone wants to join a church, they should call me because it is not my business to call them."

As I left his office that day and since then, when I reflect on the conversation, I can tell you that his philosophy was working. The church he was serving had 50 percent fewer members than it had in 1961. Have you ever wondered why "each day God added to them all who were being saved" (Acts 2:47)? It was because the members and leaders of the early church were working hard at it. Pentecost had fired the church with a fervent spirit. Three thousand had actually joined the church on the day of Pentecost (Acts 2:41). The church in Jerusalem could have easily asked, "Are we getting too big?"

Some leaders could have said "Are we only interested in numbers?" But none of that happened. They were busy in intentional ways, telling the story of Jesus Christ, his life, his death, his Resurrection, and the empowering of his spirit. People came and joined their fellowship of service and praise, and God blessed it all.

We can easily make all kinds of excuses for not working to increase the number of our members but reaching out to invite, to include, to encourage others to come, is the mission of the church. Membership matters because without membership, a commitment to Christ, what do you have? A perpetual visitor.

I love Westminster Abbey because it is a depository of English history. There you will find the tomb of the Unknown Soldier, a memorial to Sir Winston Churchill, the Poet's Corner honoring those persons who were notable for their work in literature and letters, and the memorial to John and Charles Wesley, a medallion in a place of honor. It is one of those places where you are reminded of the heritage both in faith and freedom for which we stand.

A story is told of a guide leading a group through the cathedral one day. In the group was an elderly lady from the South. She listened attentively to the sweep of history being described and the individuals of note; then she asked an essential question about Westminster Abbey. "Young man, tell me, has anyone been saved here of late?"

It is a question that every church ought to be asking about the vitality of its mission every day. Membership matters! Our proclamation of the gospel should move persons to a moment of commitment to Christ and to Christ's church. It is important that we belong. The difference between being a visitor and a member is one word: *commitment*. If you look at any of the great cathedrals in this world, they were built by commitment. It often took a century or more to finish the job but through the years, the effort was sustained by those who belonged, who were committed to raising a place of worship worthy of God. Cathedrals are not built by opinions but on convictions about Christ.

It is amazing to me how many people actually join our church who say they are joining because this is the first church they visited that asked them to join. We are living in a time when people are having a hard time making commitments that matter. The church should be one place where people are urged to make a commitment to Jesus Christ and to become members. In one of my parishes, there was a couple who had been engaged for twenty-three years. I do not know what type of relationship that was but it was not vital. It had become a sort of tired friendship and they never got married. Relationships that matter require commitment and the church should be seeking a commitment of membership for all who enter its doors.

There are many things that can be done to encourage people to join the church, making the commitment to Christ that matters. When the gospel is proclaimed, there ought to be a challenge for commitment to Christ and to membership. The fellowship of the church where you are a member should be an "inviting fellowship." We announce in the church where I serve that we receive members every Sunday. It announces to all who come that "membership matters." I cannot recall a Sunday when we did not receive new members.

I can tell you that if your church becomes a "growing church," there will be those of your members who will not like it. Several years ago, a fine member of our church came to see me to say "Why the emphasis on receiving new members? Why would we want any more members?" I asked him "Who would you turn away? Would you like to be a member of a screening committee to decide who *could* and who *could not* become a member?" He immediately changed his mind. He admitted that he had never thought about the church in that way. The church must have an open door to any and all who come and they should be challenged to make a commitment to Christ and to membership.

A Theological Imperative

I believe that church membership is a theological imperative. It begins with a commitment to Christ and it is lived out in the community of believers that is the church. Christ has promised that where we are gathered in his name that he will be with us. Our lives as members of the church are centered in Christ.

I thought President Carter was a great witness for his faith and ours when he was president. He bore a great witness for the importance of church membership when he joined a church the first Sunday he was in Washington, DC after becoming president. He joined the First Baptist Church. Someone asked him why he and Mrs. Carter did not "shop around" and visit many churches before they joined. The president said the First Baptist Church was the nearest church to the White House and that he believed that when you move the stove on which you cook to a new place, you should join a church in that place. Membership is based on a commitment to Christ, and it is a theological imperative that if you are committed to Christ, you should be a member of the church.

One of the gripping pieces of religious art is the painting entitled "Light of the World" by Holman Hunt. The original was completed in 1854 and hangs today in the chapel on the campus at Oxford University in England. John Ruskin, the critic, wrote a letter to *The London Times* in which he described the painting:

> On the left-hand side of the picture is seen this door of the human soul. It is first barred; its bars and its nails are rusty; it is knitted and bound to its stanchions by creeping tendrils of ivy, showing that it has never been opened. A bat hovers about it; its threshold is overgrown with brambles, nettles, and fruitless corn . . . Christ approaches it in the nighttime and wears the royal robe and wears the crown of thorns. In his left hand he holds a lantern, because He is the light of the world, while his right hand is raised to knock at the door.[1]

The latch on the door opens from the inside. The question that the painting raises is will someone let him in? Our membership begins with opening the door of our hearts to Christ. He is knocking on every door. Our membership, if we open the door of our hearts to him, is lived out in the community of believers: the church. There is no commitment to Christ that does not include faithful membership in the church.

A Practical Necessity

I also believe that membership matters because of practical necessity. We live out our commitment with other Christians in community; as we are together, we renew one another; we encourage each other; we support each other; we laugh together and cry together, we bear one another's burdens. The Bible calls this *koinonia*. We translate that word into English with the word "fellowship," but it is much more than that.

In the community of believers we call the church, we are living out our lives together, encouraging one another, helping to reinforce the highest instincts of the human heart toward goodness and mercy. We are more likely "to love mercy, and do justly and walk humbly before God" with the encouragement and care of others than we are in isolation. It is in the community of believers that the grand essentials of life and faith are lifted up and nourished by the spirit of Christ, to be sure, but in the life of the community as well. This happens when we worship. Look around you when you are next in church. Your very presence shows everyone "whose side you are on." You see people sitting across the aisles, singing in the choir, sitting in the balcony, just like you, just like me. It is encouraging to have the reinforcement of the presence of others.

Oliver Wendell Holmes left Harvard and enlisted in the Union Army. The Civil War was raging and on the first Sunday away from home, the soldiers were given the day off. They were camped near Washington, DC. Holmes went off to sit under a tree to write a letter home. In the letter to his parents, he told them what a comfort it was for him to sit there under that tree on Sunday morning and be able to visualize his family back home worshipping in King's Chapel in Boston. He said he could see all the people he knew would be there. He promised them that wherever the war took him, he would be found, if at all possible, in a church on Sunday worshipping. If not, he would set aside the time of day when he knew they were worshipping in the chapel back home so that he would be with them in spirit. He felt the need for the nourishing community that had shaped his life. Then he penned in his letter this great sentence: "There is a little plant called reverence within my heart and it needs watering at least once a week."

When we worship together, we are nourishing our spiritual life. The presence of others all around us doing the same thing is a great encouragement. We are sustained not only by our worship but also by our study. Sunday School or Church School forces us to be more attentive to our inner life through the study of the Bible. The content of the faith is important. If we do not know what the Bible is saying, how can we experience it as "a lamp unto our feet" and "a light for our path?"

We all need encouragement and reinforcement in our spiritual journey. The church is equipped in head and heart to share that journey. Worship will strengthen us, the study of the Bible will deepen our lives and we will be encouraged to pray. If you will study the book of Acts carefully, you will note the central role of prayer in the life of the community of believers (Acts 2:42). Prayer is encouraged to be the steady habit of our lives. Madeleine L'Engle, the poet, wrote: "In prayer the stilled voice learns to hold its peace, to listen with the heart."

When the church was born at Pentecost, it immediately began to have members as God intended. They began to do things together at once that made them even stronger: they worshipped, they studied, they prayed, and they were drawn to service and sharing. They shared what they had with one another and with others. A vital church is always reaching out to help others. And one of the most effective ways we proclaim the gospel is by reacing out to help others. Once or twice a year, we have an 18-wheel tractor trailer at our church site and we encourage our members to fill it up with all the things they would like to share with others.

When we do this, we fill trailer after trailer with useful things that we contribute to The Atlanta Union Mission. We all feel good about this because we are not helping an institution; we are helping people.

A Life of Contagious Joy

Membership in the church is *a life of contagious joy*! Read the entire book of Acts during one week. It is a stirring drama of how the church emerged and expanded onto the pages of history. There was something contagious about its life. The pagan world looked on and they wanted to know the secret. The early believers kept telling the story, proclaiming the gospel, and the church grew and grew and grew!

One of the tragic things that has happened to the church and its people is that we have allowed others to tell the world who we are. Our life together as Christians should be the most telling proof of who we are and what we are about. The early church was made up of *real* people: some good, some not so good. A couple dropped dead in church because they had not told the truth about their pledge (an event that would certainly hold the concentration of the average parish on pledge Sunday). In spite of the shortcomings and the humanity of its members, however, the church on the pages of the book of Acts is characterized by joy and joy is contagious. Jesus had promised them that it would be. He said that if they really loved one another that others would know they were his disciples. According to the Bible, "The whole city was favorable to them" (Acts 2:47).

A community of joy is contagious. I believe that in the heart of God there is joy. Karl Barth said that "the church exists . . . to set up in the world a new sign which is radically dissimilar to the world's own manner and which contradicts it in a way which is full of promise." If the church cannot be a community of joy when the world is reeling from crisis to crisis and when life is filled with the bleak, the sordid, and the violent, why would anyone turn aside to investigate who we are? Our very life together in its quality and its joy should be of such power that others will be drawn to us and there find the source of our joy. Jesus Christ who overcame the world and all it could do, said ". . . Father, forgive them for they know not what they do." He then rose to new life which he offers to you and to me.

At the risk of sounding like a preacher, I would like everyone who reads this book to join the church and to make a profession of faith in Jesus Christ, if you have not already done so, for three reasons:

1. *Do it for Christ's sake.* For his sake by joining the church, we join hands with billions around the world to do his work.

2. *Do it for our sake.* We are sinners in need of grace. Only Christ can make "all things new" in your life and in mine. A young man went to one of our church retreats. When he got back, he said "Jesus Christ is now real to me."

3. *Do it for the sake of others.* You are bearing a witness already but when you become a believer, you are bearing a witness to others for Christ. Your hesitation and procrastination may, in fact, be a barrier to another now.

It is time, past time, for many of the people who are sitting in our churches who have not joined to be asked to do so. It is time to move from being an observer to becoming a participant, from a person hesitant to a person involved. We have in our church what we call the St. Andrew's Room. It has green carpet, Scottish plaid draperies, and the flag of St. Andrew on display. It is there because we are celebrating our Scottish heritage; but more importantly, we are remembering the disciple of our Lord who was always introducing new people and bringing people to meet Jesus Christ. If we are to claim the full promise of who we are in our churches, we must produce people, who , like Andrew, find joy in introducing people to Jesus Christ. Those who have been introduced then have a decision to make. A commitment confronts them: what will you do with this Jesus?

For Reflection and Discussion

1. How many unchurched people do you know?

2. How many people have you invited to church this year?

3. Have you ever led anyone to Christ?

4. List ten unchurched people you would like to personally invite to church this year.

Epilogue

"The Grace of the Lord Jesus Christ be with you all" (Revelation 22:21)

It is appropriate that the Bible ends with Revelation 22:21. It is a blessing. The only Disciple who died a natural death, John, the Beloved Disciple, asks God's grace upon us all. It is my hope that this little volume will be a blessing upon all who read it, think upon its message, and have a clearer focus of our mission as persons and as a church.

We can be a stronger, clearer, more powerful witness for Christ than we have been. But only by the grace of God.

One of the treasured moments of my life was on an occasion when I represented our church as the fraternal delegate to the General Assembly of The Church of Scotland. In a break in the proceedings, I was invited to the Moderator's rooms and while there, met Lord George McLeod, a former Moderator who was the principle person in the restoration of Iona. I heard him speak just minutes before on the floor of the assembly against nuclear armaments and weapons. It was a passionate and moving speech. His face was lined, his hair white, and the weight of his years showed, but there was life and fire in his eyes.

I want to end by relating something Lord George McLeod said in a piece entitled "Lift High The Cross."

"I simply argue that the Cross should be raised at the center of the marketplace as well as on the steeple of the church. I am recovering the claim that Jesus was not crucified in a cathe-

dral between two candles; but on a cross between two thieves; on the town's garbage
heap; at a crossroad, so cosmopolitan they
had to write his title in Hebrew and Latin and
Greek . . . at the kind of place where cynics
talk smut, and thieves curse, and soldiers
gamble. Because that is where he died. And
that is what he died about. That is where
church-men (and women) must be and what
church-men (and women) ought to be about."[1]

I will listen, church, for the story-telling to begin: for
your proclamation of the gospel to be heard.

Notes

Chapter 1   Proclamation is Our Central Task
1. Alan E. Nelson, *Leading Your Ministry* (Nashville, Tn.: Abingdon Press, 1996), 10.
2. Ibid., 10.
3. Ibid., 10.
4. Ibid., 9.
5. James W. Moore, "The Top Ten List for Graduates," in *Dimensions for Living* (Nashville, Tn.: 1997.) 95–97.

Chapter 2   We Proclaim Because Sinners Need a Savior
1.Leonard Sweet, "The Gravity of Grace." in *Homiletics*, Volume 9, Number 3. (Canton, Oh.: Communication Resources, Inc. July/September 1997), 15.
2.Langdon Gilkey, *Shantung Compound* (New York: Harper and Row, 1966), 233.
3.William H. Willimon, "Resource," Volume 24, Number 3 (Iver Grove Heights, Mn.: Logos Productions, Inc., Year A.,July, August, September 1996), 4.
4.Charles Colson, "Making The World Safe For Religion," in *Theology Today* (November 8, 1993), 33.

Chapter 3   If Your Church Ceased to Exist, Would Anyone Miss It?
1.Alan C. Klaas, *In Search of the Unchurched* (New York: The Alban Institute, Inc., 1966), 51.
2.George G. Hunter, III, *Church for the Unchurched* (Nashville, Tn.: Abingdon Press, 1966), 19.
3.Alan C. Klaas, *In Search of the Unchurched* (New York: The Alban Institute, Inc., 1966), 17.
4.Ibid., 24–31.
5.Leslie Newbigin, *The Gospel in a Pluralistic Society* (Grand Rapids, Mi.: William B. Eerdmans Publishing Company, 1987), 227–232.
6.William H. Willimon, *Pulpit Resource* (Logos Productions, (July/August/September, 1994), 22.
7.Tom Sine, "A Different Discipleship," in *Discipleship Journal* (July/ September, 1997).
8. *Professional Builder Magazine* (May, 1997).
9. Joseph Shapiro, "Can Churches Save America?" in *U.S. News and World Report* (September 9, 1996), 46–53
10. James W. Moore, "The Top Ten List for Graduates: Priorities for Faithful Living," in *Dimensions for Living* (Nashville, Tn.: 1997), 15–17.

Chapter 4   The Church's Survival in America

1.Phillip Yancey, *The Jesus I Never Knew* (Grand Rapids, Mi.: Zondervan Publishing House, 1995), 248.

2. George G. Hunter, III, *Church For The Unchurched* (Nashville, Tn.: Abingdon Press, 1996), 51–52.

3. Maxie Dunnam, *This Is Christianity* (Nashville, Tn.: Abingdon Press, 1994), 83–84.

4. Ibid., 84.

5. Robert Wuthnow, *Christianity in the 21st Century* (Oxford, England: Oxford University Press, 1993), 6.

6. Ibid., 46–48.

7. Ibid., 49.

8. Ibid., 49.

9. "A Pollster's Index of Leading Spiritual Indicators: The State of Religion in America", in *Presbyterian Outlook*, Volume 179, 5.

10. Robert Wuthnow, *Christianity in the 21st Century* (Oxford, England: Oxford University Press, 1993), 70.

11. Charles Colson.

Chapter 5   The Bible: The Source of Our Proclamation

1. Gaily White, "Reading and Believing," in *The Atlanta Journal Constitution* (July 26, 1997).

2. Ibid., July 26, 1997.

3. Peter J. Gomes, *The Good Book* (New York: William Morrow Inc., 1996), 4–5.

4. Ibid., 5.

5. Ibid., 5.

6. Warren W. Wiersbe, *The Bible Exposition Commentary* (Wheaton, Ill.: Victor Books, A Division of Scripture Press, 1989), 252.

7. Ibid., 252.

8. Charles L. Allen, *What I Have Lived By* (Old Tappan, NJ.: 1976), 23.

9. Ibid., 13.

10. Georgia Harkness, *Beliefs That Count* (Nashville, Tn.: The Graded Press, 1961), 42.

11. William H. Willimon, *Shaped By The Bible* (Nashville, Tn.: Abingdon Press, 1990), 22.

12. Charles L. Allen, p. 25.

13. Ibid., 45.

14. Michael Green, *Evangelism In The Early Church* (Grand Rapids, Mi.: Eerdmans, 1970). Quoted from Leonard Sweet, *Homiletics*, Volume 9, Number 1 (Canton, Oh.: Communication Resources, Inc., January–March, 1997), 23.

15. Ibid., 15.

16. Anne Dillard, *Holy Firm* (New York: Harper and Row, 1977), 59.

17. Ibid., 59.

18. William H. Willimon, pp. 74–75.

Chapter 6   Your Convictions About Jesus Christ are Essential

1. John R. Stott, *Basic Christianity* (Grand Rapids, Mi.: Wm. B. Eerdmans Publishing Company, 1966), 20.

2. Ibid., 22.

3. Maxie Dunnam, *This Is Christianity* (Nashville, Tn.: Abingdon Press, 1994), 35.

4. Leonard Sweet, *Homiletics*, Volume 6, Number 1 (Canton, Oh.: Communication Resources, 1994), 13.

5. ———, Volume 6, Number 2, 8

6. William H. Willimon, "He Has Been Raised," in *Preaching Resources*, Volume 12 (Jackson, Tn.: Preaching Resources, March–April, 1997), 54.

Chapter 7 Is He Really Alive?

1. Maxie Dunnam, *This is Christianity* (Nashville, Tn.: Abingdon Press, 1994), 122.

2. Leonard Sweet, *Homiletics* (Canton, Oh.: Communications Resources, April–June, 1994), 14.

3. ———, January–March, 1994, 38.

4. Ibid., 38.

5. Maxie Dunnam, *This is Christianity*, (Nashville, Tn.: Abingdon Press, 1994), 138.

6. Ann Weems, Poem "And The Glory," in *Kneeling In Jerusalem* (Louisville, Ky.: Westminster Press, 1994), 94.

Chapter 8 We Worship Regularly

1. Stuart D. Briscoe, *Fresh Air in the Pulpit* (Grand Rapids, Mi.: Baker Books, 1994), 80.

2. John Killinger, *Preaching to a Church in Crisis* (Lima, Oh.: C.S.S. Publishing Company, Inc., 1995), 85.

3. Charles R. Swindoll, *The Finishing Touch* (Dallas, Tx.: Word Publishing, 1994), 256.

4. Ann Weems, *Searching For Shalom* (Louisville, Ky.: Westminster/John Knox Press, 1991), 81.

Chapter 9 Faith—Conviction or Convenience?

1. Kathryn Lindskoog, "Bright Shoots of Everlastingness," in *Perspects*, 8 (September, 1993), 17.

2. Ibid., 17.

3. "The Confessions," St. Augustine, 9:1.

4. "Best Sermons," James Cox, ed., 285, Vol. 7, from a sermon, "A Word For All Seasons," (San Francisco: Harper, 1997).

5. "The Confessions," St. Augustine, 9:1.

Chapter 10 I Want to Proclaim the Gospel But I Need Help

1. Maxie Dunnam, *This Is Christianity* (Nashville, Tn.: Abingdon Press, 1994), 65.

2. Doug Murren, *The Baby Boomerang: Catching Baby Boomers as They Return to Church* (Ventura, Ca.: Regal Books, 1990), 162–163.

3. Leonard Sweet, *Homiletics* (Canton, Oh.: Communication Resources, January–March, 1994), 29.

4. Charles L. Allen, *The Miracle of the Holy Spirit* (Old Tappan, NY: Fleming H. Revell Company, 1974), 29.

5. "The Practical Life of Faith," in *Insight For Living* (Fullerton, Ca. and Dallas, Tx.: Word Publishing, 1989).

6. "The Practical Life of Faith," Swindoll, p. 129.
7. *Second Lieutenant's Handbook*.

Chapter 11 Do People Really Need Saving?

1. Maxie Dunnam, *This Is Christianity* (Nashville, Tn.: Abingdon Press, 1994), 108.
2. Dennis Prager, *Think A Second Time* (New York: Regan Books, A Division of Harper Collins Publishers, 1995), 4.
3. Ibid., 4–5.
4. Leonard Sweet, *Homiletics* (Canton, Oh.: Communication Resources, January–March, 1994), 50.
5. Maxie Dunnam, *This Is Christianity* (Nashville, Tn.: Abingdon Press, 1994), 49.
6. Leonard Sweet, *Homiletics* (Canton,Oh.: Communication Resources, January–March, 1994), 45.
7. Kathleen Norris and Ticknor Fields, *Dakota: A Spiritual Geography* (New York, 1993). Reprinted in Homiletics, January–March, 1994, 49.

Chapter 12 Me an Evangelist? You've Got to be Kidding!

1. William H. Willimon, *Shaped By The Bible* (Nashville, Tn.: Abingdon Press, 1990), 9–10.
2. *Pulpit Resource*, Volume 24 (July/August/September, 1996), 3.
3. Ibid., 3.
4. Michael Green, *You Must be Joking* (London, England: Hodder and Stoughton, 1976), 12–24.
5. Ibid., 25–26.
6. Ibid, 29.
7. Ibid., 42–43.
8. Ibid., 546.
9. Maxie Dunnam, *This Is Christianity* (Nashville, Tn.: Abingdon Press, 1994), 127–128.
10. Michael Green, *You Must be Joking* (London, England: Hodder and Stoughton, 1976), 74–75.

Chapter 13 When All is Said and Done, What Will be Said and Done?

1. Thomas C. Reeves, *The Empty Church* (New York: The Free Press, A Division of Simon and Schuster, Inc., 1996), 106.
2. Ibid., 181.
3. Patrick M.. Morley, *The Seven Seasons Of A Man's Life* (Nashville, Tn.: Thomas Nelson Publishers, 1995), 203.
4. John Killinger, *Preaching To A Church In Crisis* (Lima, Oh.: C.S.S. Publishing Company, Inc., 1995), 20.
5. Thomas C. Reeves, *The Empty Church* (New York: The Free Press, A Division of Simon and Schuster, Inc., 1996), 50.
6. Thomas Long, *Whispering the Lyrics* (Lima,Oh.: C.S.S. Publishing Company, Inc., 1995), 42.
7. Patrick M. Morley, *The Seven Seasons Of A Man's Life* (Nashville, Tn: Thomas Nelson Publishers, 1995), 34.
8. Ibid., 34.
9. Thomas C. Reeves, *The Empty Church* (New York: The Free Press, A Division of Simon and Schuster, Inc., 1996), 66.

10. Ibid., 60.
11. Ben Gill, "Stewardship," in *The Biblical Basis For Living* (Arlington, Tx.: The Summit Publishing Group, 1996), 222.
12. George G. Hunter, III, *Church For The Unchurched* (Nashville, Tn.: Abingdon Press, 1996), 29–32.
13. Ibid., 79–80.
14. Ibid.

Chapter 14   Membership Matters
1. Charles R. Swindoll, *Hope Again* (Dallas, Tx.: Word Publishing, 1996), 262.

Epilogue
1. George G. Hunter, III, *Church For The Unchurched* (Nashville, Tn.: Abingdon Press, 1996), 98.